Aaron cooks Italian

Aaron
cooks
Italian

Aaron Craze, the winner
of *Jamie's Chef*

This book is dedicated to my partner Nicci, my beautiful
daughters Molly and Leah, my mother-in-law Dee, my mum
Kathleen and my extended family, the team at The Cock Inn,
all of whom I love very much.

Aaron cooks Italian
by Aaron Craze

First published in Great Britain in 2008 by Mitchell Beazley,
an imprint of Octopus Publishing Group Ltd,
2–4 Heron Quays, London E14 4JP
An Hachette Livre Company
www.octopusbooks.co.uk

ISBN: 978 1 84533 416 1

A CIP record for this book is available from the British Library

Printed and bound in China by Toppan Printing Company, Limited

Set in Caecilia LT

Commissioning Editor Rebecca Spry
Senior Editor Leanne Bryan
Copy-editor Debbie Robertson
Proofreader Gillian Haslam
Indexer Diana Lecore
Art Director Tim Foster
Designer Nicky Collings
Production Manager Peter Hunt
Photographer Jason Lowe
Prop Stylist Isabel De Cordova
Home Economist Sue Henderson

9   foreword by Jamie Oliver

10   introduction

20   pasta, risotto & gnocchi

64   meat & poultry

98   fish & shellfish

126   barbecues & snacks

148   salads & antipasti

174   bread

196   desserts

220   index

224   acknowledgements

contents

foreword by Jamie Oliver

How wonderful to be writing a foreword for a graduate of the Fifteen Foundation training program. This is the first time that I have done this for an ex-apprentice and I hope it won't be the last.

Aaron is a lovely man and an inspiring chef. His recipes show how confidently he is able to work with both Italian and British food, and how he has created his own style, which is amazing.

Although age should have nothing to do with it (if anyone knows that, I do) having eaten his food, worked with him and seen him work with the new apprentices, its very obvious that Aaron has a fantastically developed palette for someone so young. He has a really interesting way of creating food that totally works.

I remember telling him that a pasta dish he had created in his head wouldn't work and being completely humbled when he made it work and explained to me exactly how and why it would work.

I also remember him as a student all those years ago. To see that he can express himself so well in this book makes me so proud.

This is a great moment, for him, his family, the Fifteen Foundation and for me personally.

And Aaron...just keep on proving me wrong!

introduction

It was only when I was sitting on the 5pm train from Braintree to Liverpool Street heading for one of my monthly 'how-are-things-going' meetings with the Fifteen Foundation that I realized how much I've achieved in the last year, and how much I have grown as a chef and, most importantly, as a person.

Not so long ago I was a trainee at Fifteen, learning how to sharpen my new knifes and make pasta – oh, and cleaning the tiles on the kitchen floor with a toothbrush on several occasions for being late. It's funny how things work out. If someone had told me when I was 15 that I would be where I am today I would have laughed my head off. I can hardly believe that in the years between then and now I've worked with Jamie Oliver, who I once only recognized as the geezer on the box who cooks for his Nan, cooked at a number of top London restaurants, travelled around Italy tasting olive oil and loads of wine and have even run my own restaurant with my own team. The AA rosette we picked up along the way was the icing on the cake.

Before Fifteen I wasn't really doing anything. When I was younger, I had no interest in food – I was too busy playing football. I didn't take much notice of what I ate as a teenager. I loved my dad's food, though. He loved to cook... roasts, curries, homemade pies and wicked stews with dumplings were his specialities. A good old traditional Sunday roast dinner was a religious event in my dad's family. My mum was never too keen on his Sunday roasts though; I think that was down to all the mess he would leave in the kitchen. When he was at a loose end, he would make fresh bread and doughnuts. Sometimes, he'd just cook stuff that he had found in the cupboard. What he made wasn't always very appetizing but, when I look back on

it, he was a naturally gifted cook. In a weird, subconscious way, I reckon that's where I got my love of food and cooking from.

I remember coming home from work one day and watching a programme on TV that seemed vaguely familiar. Then I remembered my mum going on about this chef called Jamie Oliver, and how he was going to train 15 young kids to cook and work in a restaurant that he was setting up. There was nothing else on, and my mum was quite adamant that I watch it, so I did. That programme was *Jamie's Kitchen* and it was filmed at my local college, where I had studied a couple of years before.

At the time I had no direction in my life, just a burning ambition to be somebody and to achieve something special. I certainly wasn't getting that satisfaction from carpet-fitting – although I had fun on the jobs and met some great friends, it wasn't challenging enough for me. On *Jamie's Kitchen* it wasn't the cooking that gripped me, but Jamie Oliver, the chef. He was so bubbly and enthusiastic, so passionate about food and people and he believed in the youth of today. So much so that he was willing to put up his own money and make personal sacrifices for them. That's what really grabbed me.

By the end of the series I had mixed emotions: I was totally inspired by Jamie but utterly frustrated with some of the students. They had this golden opportunity to transform their lives with a bit of hard work and commitment but most of them blew it. At the time I was living with my mum in Fulham and my girlfriend Nicci was living in Hammersmith with our first daughter, Leah. I found it a wrench, having a family but living apart from them. They deserved better and I knew I had to do something about the situation. I needed a future and a home, and I needed an opportunity like the one I'd seen on television. I'd discovered what I wanted to do: to learn, help and be passionate about something I believed in.

The following day I decided to enrol myself on a Hospitality and Catering course at the local college. I told Nicci I was going to be a chef. She didn't take me too seriously as the week before I'd wanted to be a fireman and the week before that an actor! Nicci told her mum Dee that I was taking an interest in cooking and it didn't come as much of a surprise to her as I was always stuffing my face with the lovely food she cooked for us. Nicci's mum had taught me a lot in the kitchen.

Dee sent off for an application form for a place in the new intake of trainees at Fifteen. At my interview I told them that I knew nothing about cooking or chefs, but that I wanted to learn.

Later that day I received a phone call from the college inviting me back for a second interview; I wasn't sure if I should go as I'd felt a bit out of place in the first one, knowing nothing about the industry or cooking. But Nicci practically marched me down there. Luckily for me it was the right choice; I got through to the last 30 and went to Wales for the final selection process. I became certain I wanted to be a chef on the second morning when Jamie gave the group a breadmaking demonstration. I'd watched my dad make bread at home all the time. My bread was a success, and all the other guys were impressed. I felt a sense of achievement; I felt creative; for the first time I felt like a chef.

There was no stopping me then. I put my head down for the rest of the trip and when we arrived back in London the 15 students were announced – and I was one of them! After this I attended college for 12 weeks and was awarded an NVQ in

Hospitality and Catering. I was then put on a work placement at The Ivy restaurant in Covent Garden, London. I had no idea what to expect at this point. The only clues I had were from stories I had been reading in a book called *Kitchen Confidential* by Anthony Bourdain, which had been strongly recommended to me by a fellow trainee at college.

The chefs in the book were like pirates, immortals – creatures that worked hard and played hard, sweating from dusk till dawn with only their hunger for cooking to satisfy their appetites. One quote from the book stuck in my mind: 'You are a chef, you are no longer a human being, so don't except to be treated like one'. That was a real eye-opener and a pretty big hint about what I could expect. The Ivy was busy and hard work but a brilliant experience. I was only there for two months and then it was time to start at Fifteen.

So there I was, standing in the restaurant that I'd been watching on TV only months earlier, surrounded by some of the best chefs from around the world. When I first started at Fifteen I was struggling financially and travelling from one side of London to the other at all hours. I really started to understand what *Kitchen Confidential* was driving at. But I loved the cooking and what I was doing felt important. It was the hardest time of my life: I was 24, had a one-year-old daughter, little money to live on and no home for my new family, but I was determined to make it work.

The first six months at Fifteen were the most difficult for me. I had never worked so hard before and there were times when I thought about jacking it in, taking the easy way out and going back to carpet-fitting. I had no money and was working every weekend.

At Fifteen I'd become a baker, fishmonger, butcher and award-winning pasta chef. After a year I

At Fifteen I'd become a baker,
fishmonger, butcher and
award-winning pasta chef.
After a year I graduated with
merit and was proud of what
I'd achieved.

graduated with merit and was proud of what I'd achieved. Jamie employed me at Fifteen as a commis chef and at last I was earning a bit more money. I had more responsibility and I was involved in training the new group of trainees. I loved teaching and passing on the knowledge and skills I'd learned.

Two years on, I was still at Fifteen and had been promoted twice. I chose to stay there as it was my home and I loved everything it stood for: the brilliant produce, the freedom to be creative and the opportunities.

I remember the first time I caught wind of the idea that Jamie was going to invest in a graduate to run his or her own business. Ben Arthur, a trainee from the original *Jamie's Kitchen* and a good friend of mine, overheard a conversation that took place at Jamie's offices. Even before the scheme started, I was already working out a business plan in my head. When the scheme was finally announced I was psyched up for the challenge.

I had to have this opportunity. I couldn't see myself working anywhere else in the industry, employed by some egotistical head chef who swears and shouts at everyone for no reason. It wasn't like that at Fifteen: Jamie had broken that cycle. If you made a mistake, the chef would explain where you'd gone wrong instead of shattering your confidence with abuse. That's how I wanted to run my kitchen; I believe you get more out of people that way.

The race was now on and four graduates, me among them, were picked from about 20 to go head to head in the challenge. We had to learn all about the business side of the industry and come up with a business plan that was worth investing in. It was like *Pop Idol* meets *Dragons' Den*! On the day of the pitch, it struck me that whatever happened, that

day would change my life for ever. Win or lose, only three years ago I had been a carpet-fitter and now I was a qualified chef pitching for his own restaurant. I think I was more scared of winning than losing. If I lost, I would still be a chef and enjoy what I was doing but if I won I'd be taking on more responsibility than I could ever imagine.

Our ideas were shared with the board and it was time to wait for the verdict. Jamie gathered us together and announced that I was the winner. I was speechless. I got really emotional and thought 'Yes! I've done it'. I could finally give Nicci the life she'd longed for and my children would have a better start in life than I did. I never thought it would be easy and I soon realized just what I'd let myself in for when Jamie handed me the keys to the pub and left us to it. When everyone had gone and all the fuss was over I stood outside the 400-year-old building and thought, 'Oh shit!' It was totally silent: no police sirens or the busy traffic that I was used to in London. No mum around the corner to visit for a cup of tea. Just me, Nicci, the kids and the pub.

When we finally sorted out suppliers, the refurbishment of the building, menus and, most important of all, staff, we were ready to trade. Our first night was a disaster: there were me and Luke, a graduate from Fifteen I had employed, in the kitchen; Nicci and Kerry, our first waitress, front of house; and Nicci's mum behind the bar. We didn't have a clue. For the first month we'd get up at 7am and bake bread, work all the way through the day until we'd sent the last table's food out from the kitchen, then wash the dishes. By the time we had finished it would be three o'clock in the morning.

The hardest part of setting up the business was finding experienced staff. After all the hype from the TV show, the expectations of people coming to eat at the pub were very high and there was a lot of pressure on us to succeed. They expected it to be some fine dining restaurant owned by Jamie Oliver. There we were, in the middle of the countryside, and there was no one with any catering experience on our doorstep. We had to train the staff in about two weeks. It was like Fifteen all over again, but this time I was in Jamie's shoes. It took time, but before we knew it we were knocking out some great food and the staff were taking an interest and pride in their work.

Eventually I contacted the local college and asked if they could come and assess the young chefs I had employed so they could get some recognized qualifications. It was weird, being in a position to do for them what Jamie had done for me. Very shortly we were awarded an AA rosette for outstanding food and service in the area.

Managing The Cock Inn was a steep learning curve for me and it was a time full of ups and downs. The experience taught me a lot about running a small business, and how difficult it can be to make it work, particularly in a quiet rural area. Being forced to close the pub came as a big blow to Nicci and me, especially since we'd given the venture our all and the food we'd been serving had been such a success.

I've taken away so many positive things from that period, not least a renewed respect for people who manage to make it work under difficult circumstances. Now I'm excited about the next chapter in my life.

So why am I interested in Italian food? It might sound funny but northern Italy is pretty much like England: the weather is similar, the produce is much the same and even the landscape seems familiar, apart from the grapevines and olive trees

that grow there. The real difference is that, unlike the Italians, we're slow to take advantage of all the wonderful fresh produce we grow here.

Italy is a really inspiring place for an enthusiastic young chef to visit. It was a revelation to see how passionate the Italians are about their food. Preparing and sharing food is a near-sacred ritual there. For the first time, I saw food stripped down to the basics and cooked so simply and humbly, using no more then six ingredients in even the most adventurous dishes. And what I ate there tasted fantastic. I was particularly struck by how in tune Italian cooks are with local produce. Most of the restaurants I've visited don't even have menus: you just get what is in season, cooked however the chef wants to cook it. This way you're always trying new things that you might not otherwise have chosen from a menu.

While I was in Italy I also discovered that the wine at a meal is as important as the food. I started to understand how to match wine with food, why it's so important to do this carefully, and what a difference it makes to your evening. After all, with a different glass of wine for every course in your meal the evening can last for anything up to six hours, which is a marathon compared to the couple of hours we're used to spending in a restaurant. It shows that Italian culture and social activities revolve almost entirely around the food and wine that they produce.

My visits to Italy have really opened my eyes and shaped my perception of food. It's dawned on me that, with a little more hard work and a lot of passion, I can live a similar lifestyle at home here in Britain. I hope you feel as enthused as I do when you try some of the recipes I've collected on my travels.

pasta, risotto & gnocchi

Pasta, risotto and gnocchi are three of the most versatile basic ingredients in Italian cooking. Once you have cracked the fundamentals, the possibilities are endless. Nicci, the kids and I enjoy working together at mealtimes to make different pasta shapes and fillings. Getting everyone involved makes mealtimes loads more fun for the kids – and that sense of family togetherness is very much in line with the Italian way of life.

There are thousands of different pasta shapes, many varieties of risotto rice and loads of potatoes to choose from when making gnocchi. So which are the best?

Pasta is quick and easy to prepare and there are so many different shapes and flavours to chose from. Pasta dough requires just three basic ingredients and a bit of elbow grease – and you're laughing! It is important to match the pasta shape to the sauce. Long, strand pastas are best served with smooth, thin sauces; short shaped pastas match chunky sauces that will nestle into the grooves of the pasta.

My favourite type of risotto rice is Carnaroli, which is high in starch and produces a wonderful fluffy grain with a good bite. Never rinse the rice before cooking risotto as the starch is essential in order to get that beautifully creamy result. Always use a good-quality stock as this determines the end flavour of the dish. And keep stirring!

Spunta potatoes are perfect for gnocchi; their floury texture and low water content helps to produce a lighter, fluffier dumpling. A great alternative is Maris Piper. Always bake your potatoes on a bed of coarse sea salt to release any excess moisture.

Basic egg pasta dough

Pasta dough is easy to make as you can find all the ingredients in your cupboard: flour, eggs, extra virgin olive oil and salt. If you use whole eggs and strong flour you will have a product that is a lot denser and stronger then you would if you were to use egg yolks and tipo '00' flour. The denser dough is good for ravioli, while the dough with the '00' flour is yellower in colour and a lot softer in structure. This is good for other pastas, such as those served with carbonara and vegetable sauces.

Makes 550g (1lb 4oz) pasta dough

450g (1lb) tipo '00' Italian pasta flour, plus extra for dusting
1 tbsp salt
6 large free-range eggs
2 tbsp extra virgin olive oil

1. Mix the flour and salt in a large bowl and make a well in the middle.

2. Whisk the eggs and olive oil together and pour into the hollow in the flour. Gradually stir the flour into the egg using a wooden spoon, until all the egg is roughly mixed in.

3. Turn out the scruffy dough on to a lightly floured work surface and knead vigorously, working the edges into the centre, until all the flour and egg are completely blended together and the dough forms into a smooth ball.

4. Cut into 2 balls and wrap in clingfilm. Set aside to rest in the refrigerator for 30 minutes.

5. Working straight from the refrigerator, use a pasta machine to flatten and stretch the dough. Cut the dough into manageable pieces to fit in between the rollers on the pasta machine. Dust the dough with flour every time it passes through the machine. For ravioli, pass the dough through the machine 3–4 times, for any other type of pasta, pass the dough through the machine 6–8 times. As the sheet of dough becomes thinner, the pasta develops a soft silky-smooth consistency. The pasta dough should be rolled out to a thickness of about 2mm ($\frac{1}{16}$ in).

Tagliatelle with minute steaks rolled with Pecorino and thyme

Serves 6

½ x Basic egg pasta dough
(*see* page 25)

6 minute steaks, about 175g
(6oz) each

salt and pepper

150ml (¼ pint) extra virgin
olive oil

100g (3½oz) Pecorino Sardo,
grated

1 bunch of thyme, leaves only

6 woody sprigs of rosemary, leaves
stripped off

2 red onions, thinly sliced

4 garlic cloves, thinly sliced

pinch of chilli flakes

4 tbsp tomato purée

250ml (9fl oz) red wine

500ml (18fl oz) hot chicken stock

2 x 400g cans Italian chopped
tomatoes

50g (1¾oz) butter

1 handful of chopped flat leaf
parsley

To serve

grated Pecorino Sardo

extra virgin olive oil

When I was training at Fifteen, I was fortunate enough to work alongside Gennaro Contaldo, Jamie Oliver's mentor, who is the king of making something out of nothing. He cooked off-cuts of lamb for this dish and proved that they could taste better than the choicest cuts. I've used minute steaks but you could also use thin slices of lamb or venison.

Preheat the oven to 180°C/350°F/gas mark 4.

Roll out the pasta dough to about 2mm (¹⁄₁₆ in) thick and cut into tagliatelle. Set aside in the refrigerator.

Bat out each steak to a thin sheet with a rolling pin. Season the steaks and rub with 3 tbsp of the extra virgin olive oil. Lay the steaks on a chopping board and sprinkle with the Pecorino and thyme. Roll up and secure each with a sprig of rosemary.

Heat the remaining olive oil in an ovenproof sauté pan over a high heat and brown the steak rolls. Remove and set aside.

Turn down the heat and add the onions, garlic and chilli flakes to the pan. Sweat until softened (10–15 minutes).

Stir in the tomato purée and cook for 1–2 minutes. Turn up the heat and deglaze with the red wine. Boil to reduce the wine then add the stock and tomatoes. Return the steak rolls to the pan, cover with a lid and braise in the oven for 1 hour. Check the liquid regularly and top up with stock if necessary.

Towards the end of the cooking time, bring a large saucepan of lightly salted cold water to the boil. Add the tagliatelle and cook for 2 minutes, gently stirring with a wooden spoon to keep the pasta ribbons separate.

When the steak is tender, remove from the sauce with a slotted spoon. Discard the rosemary and cut the steak rolls into 1cm (½ in) slices. Stir the meat back into the sauce and season to taste. Drain the tagliatelle and toss in the sauce with the butter and parsley. Serve immediately with grated Pecorino and extra virgin olive oil.

Rigatoni with Italian sausages and grilled red peppers

It might sound funny but I discovered this dish while watching a gangster film. There was the usual set up: big boss man asks the chef to cook him something special tonight; cut to scene of chef knocking up this pasta dish. It looked great then and, you know what, it tastes great now.

Serves 4–6

4 large red peppers

8 Italian sausages or other strongly flavoured sausages

6 tbsp extra virgin olive oil

2 garlic cloves, finely sliced

1 red chilli, deseeded and chopped

1 tbsp fennel seeds, lightly toasted in a dry frying pan

1 x 200g can Italian chopped tomatoes

100ml (3½ fl oz) chicken stock

400g (14oz) rigatoni

1 bunch of fresh basil, leaves only

salt and pepper

Parmesan cheese for grating

Preheat the grill until very hot. Grill the peppers, gradually turning around until the skins are blackened all over. Place the charred peppers in a large bowl, cover with clingfilm and leave to sweat for 15 minutes. When cool, peel the blackened skins from the peppers. Cut the softened red peppers in half and remove the stalks, seeds and pith. Then tear each half lengthways into thin strips.

Bring a large saucepan of lightly salted cold water to the boil.

Skin the sausages and break the meat into small pieces like meatballs. Heat the olive oil in a large sauté pan and fry the sausage pieces with the garlic, chilli and fennel seeds over a medium heat until the sausagemeat is browned (about 10 minutes). Stir in the red peppers, tomatoes and chicken stock and simmer over a low heat for about 10 minutes.

Meanwhile, cook the pasta in the boiling water until *al dente* (about 9 minutes). Drain and stir into the sauce. Tear in the basil leaves and season to taste.

Serve with a wedge of Parmesan to grate over the pasta.

Big Al's spicy pork meatballs with stracci

Serves 4

400g (14oz) Basic egg pasta dough
(*see* page 25, but substitute
half the tipo '00' flour with
chestnut flour)

durum wheat semolina for dusting

2 garlic cloves, crushed

1 red chilli, deseeded and
finely chopped

150ml (¼ pint) double cream

50g (1¾oz) Parmesan cheese,
grated

extra virgin olive oil for drizzling

For the meatballs

8 good-quality pork sausages

25g (1oz) fennel seeds, lightly
toasted in a dry frying pan

20g (¾oz) dried chilli flakes

100g (3½oz) Parmesan cheese

1 sprig of rosemary, leaves only,
chopped

handful of flat leaf parsley, leaves
only, chopped

6 large free-range egg yolks

salt and pepper

3 tbsp extra virgin olive oil

100g (3½oz) unsalted butter

For me, the obvious choice of pasta to serve with meatballs would be spaghetti but the Italians are particular about which pasta they choose to match which sauce. Spaghetti is usually dried and doesn't soak up sauce as well as fresh pasta. Large triangular sheets of fresh pasta, known as stracci, hold their own better against the meatballs and their sauce.

Roll out the pasta dough into long sheets and cut into triangular stracci. Set aside on a little semolina to dry.

Fill a large saucepan with lightly salted cold water and bring to the boil.

To make the meatballs, squeeze the sausagemeat out of the sausage skins into a mixing bowl. Mix in the fennel, chilli flakes, Parmesan, rosemary and half the parsley. Then mix in 2 of the egg yolks, season the sausage mix and roll it into small meatballs.

Heat 2 tbsp of the olive oil and half the butter in a frying pan and fry the meatballs until browned all over. Then set aside to drain in a sieve.

Heat the remaining oil in a large saucepan and return the meatballs to the pan. Add the garlic and red chilli and fry over a low heat until cooked through.

Whisk the remaining egg yolks with the cream and parsley in a jug.

Blanch the pasta in the boiling water for 4 minutes, then drain through a colander, catching the water in a bowl underneath, and tip the pasta over the meatballs. Add a tbsp of the pasta water and stir well.

Pour in the whisked egg yolk mixture, stirring rapidly over a low heat until the egg thickens enough to coat the meatballs and pasta.

Taste, adjust the seasoning if necessary and serve immediately, before the egg curdles, with the grated Parmesan and drizzles of extra virgin olive oil.

Lasagnette with Parma ham, artichokes and mascarpone

Serves 4–6

1 x Basic egg pasta dough
(*see* page 25)
25g (1oz) unsalted butter

Parma ham and artichoke sauce
4 large purple artichokes
juice of 2 lemons
2 tbsp olive oil
25g (1oz) unsalted butter
12 slices of Parma ham, torn
roughly by hand
75ml (2½ fl oz) dry white wine
4 tbsp mascarpone cheese
150ml (¼ pint) hot vegetable stock

To serve
1 bunch of mint, leaves only,
chopped
Parmesan cheese for grating

There's something extra special about the marriage between mascarpone and salty meats: they complement each other so well. Fresh purple artichokes are easy to find but artichoke hearts in oil, available from your local Italian deli, work well in this dish too. And you can serve the sauce with pasta ribbons of different widths, if you like, such as tagliatelle or pappardelle.

Bring a large saucepan of lightly salted cold water to the boil.

To make the sauce, peel back about 4 layers of the outer artichoke leaves until you reach the soft and slightly yellow inner leaves. Cut the artichokes in half and remove the hairy chokes with a teaspoon. Rub the artichokes with lemon juice to stop them discolouring and slice very thinly.

Heat a large sauté pan over a medium heat and add the olive oil and butter. Once the butter has melted, fry the Parma ham and artichoke slices until the ham is crisp and the artichokes have some colour.

Add the white wine and mascarpone and cook for 3–4 minutes before pouring in the vegetable stock. Reduce the heat to minimum and leave to simmer gently.

Roll out the pasta to about 2mm (1/16 in) thick. Cut into squares of lasagnette about 7cm (2¾in) wide and 13cm (5in) long. Cook in the boiling water for 2–3 minutes. Before draining, stir in the butter to give each square a lovely gloss. Gently fold the lasagnette into the sauce.

Sprinkle the mint on top and serve immediately with the Parmesan for grating.

Ravioli pincia with slow-roasted rabbit filling

Serves 6

1 x Basic egg pasta dough
(*see* page 25)
extra virgin olive oil for drizzling

Rabbit filling

1 whole rabbit, skinned, gutted
and jointed by a butcher
3 tbsp olive oil
4 garlic cloves, thinly sliced
1 bunch of thyme
1 sprig of rosemary
8 bay leaves
1 white onion, chopped
1 celery stick, chopped
1 leek, cleaned and chopped
salt and pepper
150g (5½ oz) butter
500ml (18fl oz) white wine
100ml (3½ fl oz) chicken stock
100g (3½ fl oz) mascarpone cheese
150g (5½ oz) Parmesan cheese,
grated
1 tbsp thyme leaves
1 tbsp finely chopped rosemary
leaves
salt and pepper

I enjoyed this dish at a family vineyard in Piedmont a few years ago. *Pincia* means 'pinch' and you do exactly what it says. It's one of the smallest filled pastas, about the size of a thumbnail. Rabbit is a very popular filling in Italy.

For the rabbit filling, rub the rabbit pieces all over with 1 tbsp of the olive oil and the garlic. Spread the bunch of thyme, rosemary sprig and bay leaves over the bottom of a large baking dish. Place the rabbit on top in a single layer. Cover the baking dish and put it in the refrigerator to marinate for at least 4 hours, preferably overnight, turning the rabbit occasionally.

Preheat the oven to 190°C/375°F/gas mark 5.

Tip the vegetables into a roasting tin and drizzle with 1 tbsp of the olive oil.

Season the rabbit pieces. Heat the remaining tbsp of olive oil in a frying pan. The dark and light rabbit meats take different times to cook, with the dark meat taking longer. Start by browning the shoulders in the frying pan. (If in doubt, ask the butcher to identify the different parts of the rabbit.)

Place the browned shoulders on the vegetables in the roasting tin. Put in the oven and roast for a total of 35–40 minutes. Meanwhile, brown off the legs in the same frying pan and add to the roasting tin to roast for 20–25 minutes.

Brown the saddle and belly of the rabbit and transfer to the roasting tin. Give the contents of the roasting tin a good shake. Transfer the herbs from under the raw rabbit to on top, then dot with 55g (2oz) of the butter. Cover with kitchen foil before returning to the oven for 15–20 minutes.

When the rabbit pieces are cooked through, discard the herbs from the roasting tin. Set the rabbit aside to cool for about 20 minutes. Tip the vegetables into a bowl and set aside.

To deglaze the roasting tin, pour in the wine and stock. Simmer over a high heat for 5–10 minutes. Pass the juices through a sieve into a bowl and set aside.

When the rabbit is cool enough to handle, strip the meat off the bones and put in a food processor. Add the roasted vegetables, mascarpone, 100g (3½oz) of the Parmesan, the extra thyme and rosemary leaves. Season and blend thoroughly. Transfer the paste to a large piping bag fitted with a large plain nozzle.

To prepare the ravioli pincia, roll the pasta into sheets on setting 1 on a pasta machine. Make a ravioli shape the size of a ten-pence piece, pipe in the filling, then fold in half and pinch the two corners together to give a little pouch. Alternatively, prepare classic square-shaped ravioli as shown.

Bring a large saucepan of lightly salted cold water to the boil. Drop in the ravioli and cook the pasta for 3 minutes.

Meanwhile, melt the remaining butter in a large frying pan with a pinch of salt and pepper. When bubbling, add 3 tbsp of the boiling pasta water to the reserved stock and pour into the butter, shaking the pan to emulsify the sauce.

Drain the pasta. Tip into the sauce and toss gently to cover evenly. Serve immediately with the remaining Parmesan and a drizzle of extra virgin olive oil.

Tagliarini with lobster, lemon, parsley and purple basil

Serves 4

½ x Basic egg pasta dough
(*see* page 25)

2 tbsp durum wheat semolina

50g (1¾ oz) butter

Tuscan extra virgin olive oil,
for drizzling

Court bouillon

1 carrot, sliced

1 celery stick, sliced

1 leek, cleaned and sliced

1 Spanish onion, sliced

1 star anise

fennel tops (optional)

125ml (4fl oz) white wine

1 tbsp white wine vinegar

1 unwaxed lemon, sliced

5 bay leaves

Lobster sauce

2 live lobsters, about 550g
(1lb 4oz) each

salt and pepper

1 tbsp olive oil

1 chilli, deseeded and finely
chopped

2 garlic cloves, finely chopped

125ml (4fl oz) white wine

200ml (7fl oz) fresh or canned
lobster bisque or fresh fish stock

1 small bunch of purple or green
basil, leaves only, torn

1 small bunch of flat leaf parsley,
finely chopped

juice of ½ lemon

Tagliarini is the narrowest of ribbon pastas, a very fine stranded tagliatelle. It's very good for pasta dishes that have a lot of sauce because it absorbs the flavours really well.

Keep the lobsters in the refrigerator before killing them. (This subdues them and makes killing them slightly more humane.) Alternatively, ask the fishmonger to kill them.

For the court bouillon, put the ingredients in a large saucepan and pour in enough cold water to cover the lobsters later. Bring to the boil, reduce the heat and simmer for 45 minutes.

Meanwhile, roll the pasta dough to about 2mm (⅟₁₆ in) thick and shred into tagliarini. Dust the strands of pasta with semolina and set aside in the refrigerator.

When the bouillon is boiling, drop in the lobsters and simmer for 8 minutes. Take the saucepan to the sink and run cold water up the side until cool. Lift out the lobsters and twist off the tails. Lay each tail on its side and press down firmly until the shell cracks. Tear open the shell and remove the meat.

Pull off the claws and crack the shells by tapping with the back of a heavy knife on both sides. Scrape out the claw meat and discard any cartilage. Roughly chop the meat and season.

Bring a large saucepan of cold salted water to the boil.

To prepare the sauce, heat the olive oil in a saucepan over a medium heat. Add the lobster meat, chilli and garlic and stir-fry for 3–4 minutes. Deglaze the pan with the wine and bisque or fresh fish stock. Stir well and boil to reduce slightly (2–3 minutes). Sprinkle in the herbs and take off the heat.

Drop the pasta into the boiling water, stir and cook for 60–75 seconds. Stir the butter into the hot water before draining.

Add lemon juice and salt to the sauce to taste. Tip in the pasta and toss. To serve, divide between 4 bowls, using a long fork to twist up neat nests of the tagliarini. Drizzle with olive oil.

Cappelletti filled with prawns and chilli

Serves 6–8

400g (14oz) Basic egg pasta dough
(*see* page 25)

durum wheat semolina for dusting

100g (3½oz) unsalted butter

Spicy prawn sauce

25g (1oz) butter

15 raw tiger prawns, shelled
(save the shells) and deveined

1 tbsp tomato purée

125ml (4fl oz) white wine

½ cinnamon stick

1 star anise

250ml (9fl oz) cold water

Prawn and chilli filling

1 tbsp olive oil

1 red onion, finely chopped

2 garlic cloves, crushed

juice and rind of 1 unwaxed lemon

1 red chilli, deseeded and finely
chopped

1 tbsp extra virgin olive oil

1 small bunch of mint, leaves only,
finely chopped

salt and pepper

To serve

½ stick of bottarga (dry cured
mullet roe), grated (optional)

1 handful of flat leaf parsley,
chopped

extra virgin olive oil for drizzling

Cappelletti means 'priest's hat' and looks like a tiny bishop's mitre. Like agnolotti and tortellini, it is always best filled with fish, shellfish or cheese as its shape stops the delicate filling from escaping when the pasta is boiled.

For the sauce, melt the butter in a large saucepan, add the prawn shells and fry until turning pink. Add the tomato purée and cook for 2–3 minutes, stirring all the time. Add the wine and stir to deglaze the saucepan. Add the spices and water and simmer gently for 20 minutes. Set aside.

For the filling, heat the olive oil in a frying pan and sweat the onion and garlic over a low heat until softened (15 minutes). Blend the prawns with the lemon juice and rind in a food processor to form a coarse paste. Tip into a mixing bowl and mix in the onion, garlic, chilli, extra virgin olive oil and mint. Season to taste and set aside.

Roll the pasta out into a long narrow strip on the number 1 setting on the pasta machine. Keep the work surface dusted with a little semolina to stop the pasta sticking.

Space teaspoons of the filling well apart along the centre of the pasta strip. Cut the pasta into squares with mounds of filling in the centre of each. Turn 1 square so a corner is facing you and fold the pasta across the middle, trapping as little air as possible. Match bottom corner to top corner to form a neat triangular parcel. Press along the edges to seal. With a thumb, push the ball of filling up a little and pull the other 2 corners across each other to make the cappelletti shape. Repeat with all the pasta squares. Bring a saucepan of lightly salted cold water to the boil. Drop in the pasta and cook for 4 minutes.

Meanwhile, strain the spicy prawn sauce through a sieve into a saucepan and heat gently. Melt the butter in a large saucepan until foaming. Drain the cooked pasta and tip into the foaming butter with the hot sauce.

Serve immediately in bowls with the bottarga (if you're able to find it and brave enough to try it), a sprinkling of parsley and a drizzle of extra virgin olive oil.

Chintora filled with butternut squash and black figs

Serves 4

400g (14oz) Basic egg pasta dough (*see* page 25)
100g (3½oz) unsalted butter
8 large sage leaves

Butternut squash filling

½ butternut squash, cut in half and deseeded
1 tbsp runny honey
1 tbsp extra virgin olive oil
salt and pepper
3 sprigs of thyme, leaves only
50g (1¾oz) Amaretti biscuits
100g (3½oz) mascarpone cheese

Black fig filling

1 trevisiano or ½ radicchio, quartered and core removed
6 black figs, tops removed, cut into quarters
1 tbsp olive oil
2 tbsp aged balsamic vinegar
20g (¾oz) unsalted butter
juice and rind of 1 orange

To serve

50g (1¾oz) Parmesan cheese, grated
1 tbsp extra virgin olive oil

Chintora means 'five raviolis' and is excellent for showing off your pasta-making skills. Alternate between the two fillings given here to fill the raviolis in a strip of five.

Preheat the oven to 180°C/350°F/gas mark 4.

Cut a cross-hatch pattern into the flesh of the squash. Rub in half the honey and all of the oil and season. Place on a baking sheet lined with baking paper and roast for 45 minutes. After this time, brush the squash with the remaining honey, sprinkle over the thyme and roast for a further 10 minutes.

Meanwhile, fry the trevisiano or radicchio in a dry heavy-based frying pan. When the leaves are wilted and slightly charred, add the figs and the oil and fry for a few minutes before adding the balsamic vinegar, 1 tbsp of water and the butter. Then add the orange juice and rind. Simmer the mixture until reduced and sticky like jam. Set aside to cool.

Scoop out the flesh from the squash while still hot and blend to a smooth purée in a food processor. With the motor still running, add the Amaretti biscuits and mascarpone.

Season both the fig and the butternut squash fillings to taste.

Put a saucepan of lightly salted cold water on to boil.

Roll out the pasta into a long sheet and cut the strip in half lengthways. Space teaspoons of the fillings along one strip of the pasta. Lay the second long strip of pasta over the top and press down lightly on each little ball. Close them, expelling any air that may become trapped. Cut into belts of five joined ravioli and cook in the boiling salted water for 3 minutes.

Meanwhile, melt the butter in a large frying pan and fry the sage until the butter foams. Then stir in about 3 tbsp of pasta water, a spoonful at a time, until you have a butter emulsion. Transfer the cooked pasta to the butter emulsion and coat well. Serve a belt of 5 ravioli to each person with grated Parmesan and a drizzle of extra virgin olive oil.

Linguini with fresh tomatoes, green olives and mozzarella

Simple! Simple! Simple! What more can I say, apart from that it's delicious. *Linguini Sorentina*, as this rustic dish is known in Italy, combines all the basics of Italian cooking: tomatoes, olives, garlic, oregano and spaghetti-type pasta.

Serves 4–6

100ml (3½ fl oz) extra virgin olive oil, plus extra for drizzling
4 garlic cloves, finely sliced
1kg (2lb 4oz) cherry tomatoes
1 tsp caster sugar
1 bunch of oregano, leaves only
400g (14oz) green olives, pitted and roughly chopped
500g (1lb 2oz) mozzarella cheese, torn into small pieces
400g (14oz) dried linguini
salt and pepper
grated Parmesan cheese, to serve

Bring a large saucepan of lightly salted cold water to the boil.

In another large saucepan, heat the olive oil over a medium heat. Add the garlic and tomatoes and fry for 20 minutes, stirring frequently.

When the tomatoes have softened and collapsed, crush some with a potato masher to release more juices. Then stir in the sugar, oregano, olives and half the mozzarella.

Drop the linguini pasta into the boiling water and cook until *al dente* (about 9 minutes). Drain and tip into the tomato sauce. Add the remaining mozzarella and fold together well so that the pasta soaks up the sauce and the cheese warms through. Season to taste.

Serve with the Parmesan and a drizzle of extra virgin olive oil.

Agnolotti of roasted red onion, pine nuts, rocket and Anya potatoes

Makes 25 agnolotti

½ x Basic egg pasta dough
(*see* page 25)
durum wheat semolina for dusting
1 tbsp butter

Filling

1 medium red onion, quartered

6 tsp balsamic vinegar

1 small handful of thyme leaves

2 tbsp olive oil

salt and pepper

200g (7oz) Anya potatoes,
parboiled, skinned and crushed

1 large handful of grated
Parmesan cheese

1 small handful of pine nuts,
lightly toasted in a dry frying pan

1 large handful of chopped rocket

3 tbsp extra virgin olive oil

This is my favourite vegetarian pasta, packed with strong flavours and extremely satisfying. I've chosen Anya potatoes because they're very waxy and their skins have loads of nutty flavour. I also find that the sweet red onion contrasts beautifully with the peppery rocket.

Preheat the oven to 200°C/400°F/gas mark 6.

To prepare the filling, put the onion, balsamic vinegar and thyme in a roasting tin and drizzle over the olive oil. Season with salt and pepper. Cover with a piece of wet baking paper and roast in the oven until the onion is softened (20 minutes).

Chop the onion into a mixing bowl and stir in the potatoes, Parmesan, pine nuts, rocket and 1 tbsp of the extra virgin olive oil.

Roll the pasta into a sheet about as large as 2 pieces of A4 paper laid end to end. Then place teaspoonfuls of the filling on to the pasta, leaving a gap about 2 fingers wide between each mound.

Bring a saucepan of lightly salted cold water to the boil.

Use a large round pasta cutter to stamp out discs with the filling in the centre of the pasta sheet. Then fold one side of the pasta disc over the filling to make a half-moon shape. To shape the agnolotti, fold the semicircular edge up and pinch the 2 corners together to make each piece look like a baby's bonnet.

Cook the stuffed pasta in the boiling salted water until the agnolotti rise to the surface (about 3 minutes), then drain.

Melt the butter in a saucepan. When it starts to colour, stir in 1 tbsp of water and shake the saucepan to make the sauce. Remove from the heat, stir in the agnolotti and serve straight away.

Many hands make light work when shaping a batch of agnolotti. It speeds things up no end to organize a sort of production line: one person to spoon on the filling, another to stamp out the pasta; then one folds and the other pinches.

Ravioli soleil with asparagus and Pecorino

Serves 4

200g (7oz) Basic egg pasta dough
(*see* page 25)
durum wheat semolina for dusting
100g (3½oz) unsalted butter

Asparagus filling
15 asparagus spears, woody stalks
removed, stems and tips separated
salt and pepper
100g (3½oz) Pecorino Sardo,
grated
70g (2½oz) mascarpone cheese
juice and rind of ½ unwaxed lemon
2 tsp extra virgin olive oil
4 large free-range egg yolks

To serve
50g (1¾oz) Parmesan cheese or
Pecorino Sardo for grating
extra virgin olive oil for drizzling
white truffle oil (optional)

I ate this wonderful dish on my first trip to Tuscany and thought that the rich runny yolk flowing into the butter and asparagus sauce was fantastic. On that occasion it was served on its own but I love to serve it with some shavings of pecorino and an extravagant drop or two of truffle oil.

Bring 2 saucepans of lightly salted cold water to the boil.

Blanch the asparagus stems and tips for 4 minutes in 1 saucepan. Drain, season well with salt and pepper and set the tips aside.

Blitz the asparagus stems, Pecorino, mascarpone, lemon juice and rind and olive oil in a food processor. Taste and adjust the seasoning if necessary, remembering that you should always season pasta fillings generously.

Divide the pasta dough into 8 equal balls and roll out into 8 square sheets on the number 1 setting on a pasta machine. Place a tbsp of the filling into the centre of 4 of the sheets. Make a small well in the middle of each mound of filling, without exposing the pasta underneath. Gently place an egg yolk in each hollow and season each yolk. Close each ravioli with a second matching sheet, expelling any air so the pasta and filling can cook properly. Set aside on a tray dusted with semolina.

Poach the ravioli for 3 minutes in the second saucepan of boiling water.

Meanwhile, melt the butter in a large heavy-based frying pan. Add the asparagus tips and fry briefly to warm through.

Drain the pasta, saving a little cooking water, and tip into the butter. Add a little of the pasta cooking water to the saucepan to make a butter sauce.

Serve immediately with grated cheese, a drizzle of extra virgin olive oil and a few drops of white truffle oil, if you're feeling extravagant.

Penne with sun-blushed tomato pesto

The first time I ever tasted real Italian cooking was in Fulham Broadway in a little deli that, sadly, no longer exists. My friend used to go there for lunch and took me along once. I had this dish with homemade garlic bread, extra virgin olive oil and heaps of grated Parmesan. It's still my first choice for lunch when it's on offer.

Serves 4

500g (1lb 2oz) dried penne

Sun-blushed tomato pesto
300g (10½oz) sun-blushed tomatoes
1 bunch of basil, leaves only
100g (3½oz) pine nuts, lightly toasted in a dry frying pan
4 tbsp grated Parmesan cheese
juice of 1 lemon
salt and pepper
extra virgin olive oil

To prepare the sun-blushed tomato pesto, blend the tomatoes and most of the basil to a smooth paste in a food processor. Add the pine nuts, Parmesan, lemon juice and a little salt and pepper. Continue to blend while adding just enough olive oil to bind everything into a soft paste. (If you want to make the sun-blushed tomato pesto in advance, just leave out the Parmesan. Then you can keep it in an airtight sterilized jar in the refrigerator for about a month. Add the Parmesan when you're ready to use the pesto.)

Bring a large saucepan of cold salted water to the boil. Drop in the penne and cook until soft but still *al dente* (about 9 minutes).

When the penne is cooked, drain and return to the saucepan. Stir in the sun-blushed tomato pesto so that all the pasta is well coated. Serve immediately, garnished with the remaining basil leaves, roughly torn.

Basic risotto bianco

Risotto is simply toasted rice cooked with good stock to give a creamy consistency. First you heat the rice to crack the grains and make them porous. Then, as you add the stock little by little, stirring continuously, the rice gradually absorbs the liquid and swells, releasing starch that gets rubbed off and moved around to make the finished risotto beautifully creamy. The secret to any risotto is the stock it's cooked with; the more flavour and intensity in the stock, the better the finished product.

Serves 6

1 litre (1¾ pints) stock (chicken, fish or vegetable, as appropriate)
3 tbsp olive oil
1 large onion or fennel bulb, finely chopped
3 garlic cloves, finely chopped
3 celery sticks, finely chopped
400g (14oz) Carnaroli risotto rice
375ml (13fl oz) white wine
150g (5½oz) Parmesan cheese, grated
60g (2¼oz) unsalted butter
1 bunch of flat leaf parsley, finely chopped

1. Pour the stock into a saucepan and bring to the boil, then cover and set aside to keep hot.

2. Heat the olive oil in a large sauté pan. Add the onion or fennel, garlic and celery. Sweat over a medium heat until the vegetables are softened (5–10 minutes).

3. Add the risotto rice and cook for about 6 minutes, stirring continuously with a wooden spoon, until the grains are translucent.

4. Pour in the white wine and keep stirring until absorbed. Then start adding the hot stock, a ladle at a time, stirring continuously over a medium–low heat. Wait until each ladle of stock has been absorbed by the rice before adding the next.

5. Continue adding the stock for about 15 minutes. Check the rice regularly to see if it is cooked. Lift out a grain and squeeze it between your fingers: when there is only a tiny speck of white core left, the rice is ready.

6. Remove from the heat and stir in the Parmesan, butter and parsley. Cover with a lid and leave to rest for about 3 minutes before serving.

Chorizo sausage and red wine risotto with Gorgonzola crostini

Serves 6

600ml (1 pint) chicken stock

500g (1lb 2oz) chorizo sausage, skinned and roughly chopped.

½ Spanish onion, finely chopped

2 fennel bulbs, finely chopped

3 garlic cloves, finely chopped

1kg (2lb 4oz) sweet cherry tomatoes, cut in half

1 bottle of red wine

450g (1lb) Carnaroli risotto rice

50g (1¾oz) Parmesan cheese, grated

50g (1¾oz) unsalted butter

pinch of dried chilli flakes

1 handful of sage leaves, chopped

salt and pepper

extra virgin olive oil

Gorgonzola crostini

6 tbsp Gorgonzola dolce cheese

6 thin slices of ciabatta bread, toasted

1 garlic clove, cut in half

The first time I ate this dish was in Piedmont in Italy. The risotto was served on one side of the plate with gnocchi and Gorgonzola cheese on the other. I thought that those two dishes on the same plate were a smashing combination of flavours and I have reunited these flavours here.

Preheat the grill to medium. Pour the stock into a saucepan and bring to the boil. Remove from the heat, cover and set aside.

Add the chorizo, onion, fennel and garlic to a large sauté saucepan and fry over a high heat for 1 minute. Then reduce the heat and sweat the vegetables in the oil released by the sausage. After 3–4 minutes, add the tomatoes and continue stewing gently until the onions are softened (10–15 minutes).

Pour in 250ml (9fl oz) of the wine and boil until evaporated. Turn up the heat again and add the rice. Fry for 5 minutes, stirring continuously.

Tip in the rest of the wine and stir until all the liquid has been absorbed by the rice. Turn the heat down to medium and start adding the hot stock, a ladle at a time, stirring continuously. After 15 minutes, lift out a grain of rice and squeeze it between your fingers: the rice is ready when there is only a speck of white left through the centre.

Stir in the cheese, butter, chilli and sage. If the risotto is a little dry, stir in another ladle of hot stock so that the rice is moist and creamy. Remove from the heat, cover with a lid and set aside to rest in a warm place for 4–5 minutes.

While the risotto is resting, rub the cut face of the garlic over the toasted crostini, then spread the Gorgonzola on top and warm under the grill.

When ready to serve, give the risotto a final stir to check the consistency and season with salt and pepper to taste.

Serve on warm plates, topped with the crostini and a drizzle of extra virgin olive oil.

Ham hock, roast chestnut and balsamic vinegar risotto with crisp fried sage leaves

Serves 6

1 x Basic risotto bianco
(*see* page 45), made
without parsley

200g (7oz) roasted chestnuts,
roughly chopped

2 tbsp balsamic vinegar

Ham hock

2 raw ham hocks

3 tbsp olive oil

4 large carrots, peeled and roughly
chopped

4 celery sticks, roughly chopped

4 red onions, roughly chopped

1 garlic bulb, cut in half around
the middle

1 tbsp fennel seeds

1 chilli, deseeded and chopped

1 tbsp black peppercorns

Crisp fried sage leaves

150ml (5fl oz) vegetable oil

bunch of sage, leaves only

Bursting with flavour, this is a really good Christmas dish. The secret behind any tasty risotto lies in the quality of the stock used to make it. That's where the true body of the dish comes from. In this case, it's very important to follow the steps outlined in the recipe to prevent the ham stock from becoming too salty.

Put the ham hocks in a large saucepan, cover with cold water and bring to the boil. After 5 minutes, remove the ham hocks from the water and set aside. (This draws excess salt from the ham and gives a good balance to the stock.)

Pour the olive oil into another large saucepan, add the carrots, celery, onions and garlic and fry over a high heat until browned (about 5 minutes). Add the fennel seeds, chilli and peppercorns. Continue cooking for 1 minute to toast the spices, then add the ham hocks and pour in enough water to cover them. Bring to the boil, cover and simmer until the ham is falling off the bone (about 1½ hours). Take off the heat and set aside to let the ham cool down in the stock.

When cooled, remove all the meat from the bones and trim off any excess fat or gristle. Shred the ham and roughly chop into small pieces. Put in a bowl and set aside.

Strain the ham stock into another saucepan and boil to reduce to about 1 litre (1¾ pints). Keep warm to use later for cooking the risotto.

To prepare the fried sage leaves, heat the vegetable oil in a frying pan. When hot, carefully drop in the sage leaves and fry for a minute. Turn off the heat and use a slotted spoon to transfer the leaves to kitchen paper to absorb any excess oil.

Prepare the Basic risotto bianco, adding the chopped ham, roasted chestnuts and balsamic vinegar with the wine and using the ham stock.

Serve garnished with the crisp fried sage leaves.

Risotto with smoked eel and sorrel

Although I like to eat this hot, I always secretly hope that there'll be some slightly overcooked risotto left in the saucepan that I can cool off in the refrigerator. Later I roll the cold risotto into small balls, about the size of golf balls, that I toss in flour, dip in beaten egg, roll in breadcrumbs and fry into a great little snack.

Serves 6

1 x Basic risotto bianco (*see* page 45), made with fish stock

1 red chilli, deseeded and chopped

juice and rind of 3 unwaxed lemons

300–400g (10½–14oz) smoked eel, skinned, boned and chopped into bite-sized pieces

20 sorrel leaves, torn

salt and pepper

Prepare the Basic risotto bianco using the fish stock. Add the chilli and lemon rind in step 2.

Stir in the lemon juice, smoked eel and sorrel in step 6. There is enough heat in the risotto to warm the eel through and wilt the sorrel. Set aside to rest for 3 minutes. Season to taste and serve immediately.

Risotto with crab, cherry tomatoes and tarragon

Traditionally, Italians never put cheese in fish or shellfish risottos: I made that mistake once and my Italian chef nearly chopped my hands off. I find topping the bruschetta with some brown crabmeat adds loads of flavour to the dish.

Serves 6

1 x Basic risotto bianco (*see* page 45), using fish stock and leaving out the cheese
2 red chillies, deseeded and finely chopped
1 tsp fennel seeds, lightly toasted in a dry frying pan and crushed
6 anchovy fillets
juice and rind of 1 unwaxed lemon
pinch of saffron strands
500g (1lb 2oz) mixed yellow and red cherry tomatoes, cut in half
500g (1lb 2oz) cooked fresh white crabmeat
1 bunch of tarragon, leaves only, torn
salt and pepper

Crabmeat bruschetta

6 slices ciabatta bread
extra virgin olive oil, plus extra for drizzling
1 garlic clove, cut in half
350g (12oz) cooked fresh brown crabmeat

Prepare the Basic risotto bianco with fish stock, adding the chillies, fennel seeds, anchovies, lemon rind and saffron in step 2.

Add the tomatoes in step 4. Mix in the white crabmeat, lemon juice and tarragon in step 6. Bring the risotto gently back to the boil and simmer for 1–2 minutes to make sure the crab is well heated through. Cover and rest for 3 minutes.

Meanwhile, make the bruschetta. Brush both sides of the bread with olive oil and toast on a hot griddle until branded with clear bar marks. Rub the cut face of the garlic over the toasted slices and spread the brown crabmeat on top.

Stir the risotto to check the consistency, season to taste and serve in shallow bowls drizzled with extra virgin olive oil and accompanied by crabmeat bruschetta.

Risotto with purple cauliflower and Amalfi lemon

Look for purple cauliflower in the greengrocer's around November time. The flavour is similar to white cauliflower and if you can't find purple, white is fine. Purple is definitely prettier though. The anchovy fillets add an extra depth of flavour but, if they put you off making this luscious dish, you don't have to use them.

Serves 6

1 x Basic risotto bianco (*see* page 45)
150ml (¼ pint) red wine
juice and rind of 2 large unwaxed Amalfi lemons
pinch of chilli flakes
6 anchovy fillets (optional)
1kg (2lb 4oz) purple cauliflower, florets quartered
3 tbsp extra virgin olive oil
3 garlic cloves, chopped
salt and pepper

Prepare the Basic risotto bianco, using 150ml (5fl oz) red wine in addition to the white wine. Add the lemon rind, dried chilli and anchovies, if you like their salty kick, in step 2. Mix in the purple cauliflower in step 4 while stirring in the hot stock.

Add the lemon juice in step 6. Set aside to rest for 3 minutes. Season to taste and serve immediately.

Basic gnocchi

Most people boil the potatoes for making gnocchi but I think you lose nutrients that way and the dumplings end up being stodgy. I always bake my potatoes to keep all the goodness and flavour in. I also use '00' flour, which has been triple milled. It's much softer and finer than strong flour and helps the end result to be really light and fluffy.

Makes 550g (1lb 4oz) dough

450g (1lb) large Maris Piper or Russet potatoes
100g (3½oz) rock salt for baking
1 free-range egg
2 tbsp tipo '00' pasta flour, plain flour or durum wheat semolina
½ nutmeg, grated
1 large pinch of salt

1. Preheat the oven to 200°C/400°F/gas mark 6. Put a small saucepan of water on to boil, ready to test the gnocchi.

2. Bake the potatoes on a bed of rock salt for about 1 hour or until done.

3. While the potatoes are still hot, carefully scoop out the potato from its skin and press through a sieve, potato ricer or mouli. Set aside to cool.

4. When the potato feels warm rather than hot, mix in the egg, flour, nutmeg and salt. Knead into a fairly firm dough, adding more flour if necessary.

5. To test the consistency of the dough, pull off a small piece and blanch in the boiling water for 4–5 minutes until the gnocchi floats. If the gnocchi breaks up, add a little more flour to stiffen the dough.

6. Roll the dough into 2 sausage-shapes, about 2cm (¾ in) in diameter. Roll through flour or semolina and cut into 2.5cm (1in) pieces that look a bit like little pillows. Pinch each one lightly in the middle. Set aside in the refrigerator.

My award-winning tomato gnocchi with oxtail stew

Serves 4–6

1 x Basic gnocchi (*see* page 55)

1 tbsp tomato purée

For the oxtail stew

1 or 2 whole oxtail, about 1.25kg (2lb 12oz) each, trimmed and cut into sections by a butcher

1 pig's trotter

3 tbsp plain flour

salt and pepper

100ml (3½ fl oz) olive oil

1 onion, roughly chopped

1 celery stick, roughly chopped

½ leek, cleaned and roughly chopped

2 bulbs of garlic, cut in half around the middle

150g (5½ oz) tomato purée

1 tbsp fennel seeds

1 tbsp juniper berries

2 star anise

½ cinnamon stick

pinch of dried chilli flakes

6 bay leaves

6 sprigs of rosemary

1 bunch of lemon thyme

500ml (18fl oz) chicken stock

1.5kg (3lb 4oz) canned Italian chopped tomatoes

To serve

100ml (3½ fl oz) extra virgin olive oil

100g (3½ oz) Parmesan cheese, grated

This dish is special to me in several ways. First, it won an award for being the Best Pasta Dish in the UK from *The Restaurant Magazine*. Second, it helped me graduate from being a trainee to a respected and recognized chef, which was a great boost to my confidence and ambition.

Preheat the oven to 180°C/350°F/gas mark 4. Dust the meat in seasoned flour. Heat the olive oil in a large, flameproof casserole and fry the meat until browned. Remove and set aside. Add the vegetables and garlic to the casserole and sweat over a low heat until softened (5–10 minutes).

Stir in the tomato purée, increase the heat to medium and cook for 2–3 minutes. Return the oxtail and pig's trotter to the casserole and add the spices, berries and herbs, preferably tied up in a piece of muslin. Pour in the chicken stock. Increase the heat to high and bring the stock to simmering point before tipping in the tomatoes.

Cover with a lid or kitchen foil and put in the oven. Braise the oxtail for 3½ – 4 hours, making sure that the stew is kept topped up with stock or water to stop it becoming too dry. As soon as the oxtail starts to fall off the bone when poked with a fork, remove the pig's trotter and spice bag and discard.

Remove the oxtail pieces from the casserole with a slotted spoon. Place in a bowl and set aside for about 20 minutes to cool down slightly before picking the meat off the bones. Discard any cartilage and fat in the process.

Press the sauce through a sieve or a mouli into a saucepan and stir in the meat. Check and adjust the seasoning.

While preparing the gnocchi, add the tomato purée in step 4. Shape according to the rest of the recipe. Bring a large saucepan of cold salted water to the boil. Cook the gnocchi in the boiling water for 2–4 minutes until they rise to the surface.

Toss the drained gnocchi through the oxtail stew and serve with extra virgin olive oil and grated Parmesan.

Minted gnocchi with chicken and peas

Serves 6

1 x Basic gnocchi (*see* page 55)

1 bunch of mint, leaves only, finely chopped

For the chicken and peas

100ml (3½ fl oz) olive oil

1 whole chicken on the bone, about 900g–1kg (2lb–2lb 4oz), cut into 10 pieces

2 Spanish onions, finely sliced

1 bulb of garlic, cut in half around the middle

1 bunch of sage, leaves only

1 bunch of lemon thyme

rind of 1 unwaxed lemon, peeled into strips

1 large glass of white wine

1.4 litres (2½ pints) chicken stock

500g (1lb 2oz) fresh (shelled weight) or frozen garden peas

salt and pepper

To serve

extra virgin olive oil

100g (3½ oz) Pecorino Sardo, grated

This is probably my favourite gnocchi dish as it's so humble and full of flavour. It's classed as a peasant dish due to the simplicity of the ingredients and goes down really well with a hunk of crusty bread and loads of good extra virgin olive oil.

Prepare the Basic gnocchi (*see* page 55), adding mint in step 4.

Preheat the oven to 180°C/350°F/gas mark 4.

Heat the olive oil in a large flameproof casserole, cook the chicken pieces in batches over a high heat until well browned.

Turn the chicken pieces onto the bone side and add the onions, garlic and sage to the casserole. Tie the lemon thyme and lemon peel together with butcher's twine and add to the pot.

Turn down the heat to minimum and slowly sweat the vegetables until the onions are softened but not browned. Turn the heat up to high to steam off any residual vegetable juices. Pour in the wine: the liquid should sizzle as it hits the bottom of the pot. Boil until the wine has evaporated, then add the stock to cover the chicken. Bring to a simmer and cover with a lid. Put in the oven to braise until the chicken is still moist but falling off the bone (about 1 hour). Check the level of stock from time to time and top up if a little low.

When cooked, transfer the chicken pieces to a bowl with a slotted spoon. Set aside to cool for 20 minutes.

Lift the garlic and the bouquet of lemon thyme and lemon rind out of the casserole before placing over a medium heat. Simmer the stock until reduced by half and thickened. When nearly there, add the peas and cook for 10 minutes.

Bring a large saucepan of cold salted water to the boil.

Meanwhile, strip the chicken from the bones. When the sauce is ready, return the chicken to the casserole. Season to taste.

Cook the gnocchi in the boiling water for 2–4 minutes until they rise to the surface. Drain and stir into the chicken stew. Serve in bowls with extra virgin olive oil and grated Pecorino.

Chervil gnocchi with broad beans and mint

Serves 4

1 x Basic gnocchi (*see* page 55)

2 tbsp finely chopped chervil

Broad bean and mint sauce

350g (12oz) broad beans
(weight after podding)

2 tsp olive oil

1 red chilli, deseeded and
finely chopped

2 garlic cloves, pressed

125ml (4fl oz) white wine

100g (3½oz) unsalted butter

juice and finely grated rind
of ½ unwaxed lemon

100ml (3½fl oz) hot vegetable
stock

salt and pepper

To serve

50g (1¾oz) *Parmigiano Reggiano*,
shaved

1 handful of fresh mint, leaves
only, chopped

extra virgin olive oil

This is a lovely light dish for the summer that goes down brilliantly with a glass of chilled white wine. You can buy frozen broad beans from the supermarket if you really must, but do try to use fresh ones when they're in season: it's a bit more work but delivers a lot more pleasure.

When preparing the Basic gnocchi, add the chervil with the egg in step 4.

To make the broad bean and mint sauce, blanch the broad beans in a saucepan of lightly salted boiling water for 4 minutes and refresh under cold running water. Drain, then squeeze all the bright green beans out of their grey-green skin.

Bring a large saucepan of lightly salted cold water to the boil.

Heat the olive oil in a large heavy-based saucepan and fry the chilli and garlic over a low heat for 3–4 minutes. Throw in the skinless broad beans and mix well. Turn up the heat and pour in the wine, stirring vigorously. Let the wine evaporate before adding the butter and lemon juice and rind. As soon as the butter has melted, pour the stock into the sauce, whisking well to blend and emulsify.

Drop the gnocchi into the boiling water and cook for about 2–4 minutes until they float to the surface. Drain and stir into the sauce, giving the gnocchi a chance to absorb the flavours. Check the seasoning and adjust if necessary.

Serve immediately with the *Parmigiano Reggiano*, a sprinkling of mint and a drizzle of extra virgin olive oil.

Lemon gnocchi with mussels and clams

The word *gnocco* means 'lump' in colloquial Italian. Gnocchi are often served with pasta sauces, but they cook much faster than pasta and can fall apart if overcooked. At their best, potato gnocchi are light and delicate. At their worst, they are dense and soggy! Follow this recipe closely for the best result.

Serves 4–6

1 x Basic gnocchi (*see* page 55)
rind of 4 unwaxed lemons and 1 tbsp lemon juice

Shellfish sauce
4 tbsp extra virgin olive oil
1kg (2lb 4oz) fresh mussels, cleaned and debearded
1kg (2lb 4oz) fresh clams, cleaned and debearded
1 fresh red chilli, deseeded and finely chopped
2 garlic cloves, finely sliced
500ml (18fl oz) dry white wine
100ml (3½ fl oz) fish stock
1 bunch of flat leaf parsley, leaves only, chopped
salt and pepper

When making the Basic gnocchi, add the lemon rind at the same time as the eggs, then continue following the recipe. Set the gnocchi aside to rest. Bring a large saucepan of lightly salted cold water to the boil.

Heat the olive oil in a large sauté pan big enough to hold all the shellfish. Discard any mussels or clams that are open and fail to close when tapped against the side of the sink, and tip the remainder into the pan. Cover with a lid and cook over a high heat for about 3 minutes. Take off the lid and add the chilli and garlic. Cook for a further 3 minutes before adding the wine. When it has evaporated, pour in the fish stock and cover the pan again for another 3 minutes.

Take off the heat and pass the shellfish sauce through a sieve into another saucepan and set aside. Throw away any shellfish that have not opened. Remove most of the mussels and clams from their shells, discarding the empties, and tip back into the shellfish sauce. Place the saucepan over a low heat to keep hot. Drop the gnocchi into the boiling water and cook for 2–4 minutes until they float to the surface. Drain and tip the gnocchi into the hot shellfish sauce. Stir in the lemon juice and parsley. Season to taste and serve at once.

Gnocchi with Gorgonzola and walnuts

This dish is very typical of northern Italy, where walnuts are plump and plentiful. Their sweet flavour has a touch of bitterness on the aftertaste, which works well with Gorgonzola dolce cheese. The gnocchi dumplings soak up all the flavours, leaving you to savour the contrast of textures and tastes, one mouthful at a time.

Serves 4

1 x Basic gnocchi (*see* page 55)
100g (3½oz) Gorgonzola dolce
20g (¾oz) unsalted butter
4 tbsp double cream
cracked black pepper
100g (3½oz) walnut pieces, roughly broken up by hand

Take the Gorgonzola out of the refrigerator about an hour before cooking and let it come to room temperature for the tastiest result.

Bring a large saucepan of lightly salted cold water to the boil.

Put the butter, Gorgonzola, double cream and black pepper into a nonstick frying pan. Cook over a low heat, stirring continuously with a wooden spoon until the cheese melts and blends with the butter and cream. Remove from the heat just as the sauce starts to bubble.

Drop the gnocchi into the boiling water and cook for 2–4 minutes until they rise to the surface. Drain the gnocchi and fold into the sauce until completely coated.

Serve in bowls, sprinkled with the walnuts and more black pepper.

Parsley gnocchi with summer girolles and Pecorino

Serves 4

1 x Basic gnocchi (*see* page 55)
3 tbsp finely chopped flat leaf parsley

Mushroom sauce

500g (1lb 2oz) girolles, torn to match the size of the gnocchi

1 tbsp lemon thyme leaves, stalks reserved

2 garlic cloves, finely chopped, trimmings reserved

1 shallot, finely chopped, trimmings reserved

1 tbsp olive oil

100g (3½oz) unsalted butter

1 red chilli, deseeded and sliced

1 bay leaf

250ml (9fl oz) white wine

juice and rind of ½ unwaxed lemon

salt and pepper

To serve

100g (3½oz) Pecorino Sardo shavings

extra virgin olive oil

The delicate flavour of the girolles in this wonderful dish really gets the taste buds tingling. Make sure you clean the mushrooms thoroughly before cooking with them as they are often sold directly from the forest. Use a small pastry brush to brush off any excess dirt.

When preparing the Basic gnocchi, mix in the parsley with the egg in step 4.

Bring a saucepan of lightly salted cold water to the boil.

To make the mushroom sauce, carefully peel and trim the stalks of the mushrooms and clean the caps with a damp cloth. Put all the mushroom trimmings in a saucepan with 150ml (¼ pint) water, the lemon thyme stalks and the garlic and shallot trimmings. Simmer gently for 5–10 minutes to form a mushroom stock.

Heat up a large frying pan, add the olive oil, then turn the heat down and fry the girolles, stirring continuously with a wooden spoon. When the mushrooms are well coated in olive oil, increase the heat again and stir in the butter, garlic, shallot, chilli, bay leaf and lemon thyme.

When the butter has melted, add the wine and boil until it has almost completely evaporated.

Pass the mushroom stock through a sieve and add to the frying pan with the lemon juice and rind. Reduce until the sauce has reached the consistency of whipping cream. Pick out the bay leaf.

Drop the parsley gnocchi into the boiling water, increase the heat and boil for 2–4 minutes until they float to the surface. Drain and stir into the sauce. Check the flavour and adjust the seasoning if necessary.

To serve, share between 4 bowls and garnish with Pecorino shavings and a drizzle of extra virgin olive oil.

meat &
poultry

When buying meat, look for two things in particular: the fat content (marbling) and the colour. For the healthy option, buy lean cuts of meat – those with less marbling distributed within the lean. The darker the colour of the meat you buy, the better; this means it has been hung for the correct amount of time – about three weeks. Don't be fooled by the bright red, artificial appearance of supermarket meat. This means that the blood hasn't had enough time to discard, which can make the meat tough.

There are so many different cuts of meat to choose from, but the temptation is always to go for the easy options – steaks, fillets, legs and chops. Why not be a little more adventurous and try shoulder, tail, skirt, neck, shin – or even trotter! These cuts require slightly different methods of preparation and cooking, but as they are all on the bone they offer a more intense flavour. They are perfect cooked slowly in stews, casseroles, braised or even just slow roasted.

Rolled loin of pork stuffed with dried apricots and sage

Serves 6–8

½ pork loin with belly, about 2.5kg (5lb 8oz), boned

2 tsp sea salt crystals

115ml (3¾ fl oz) olive oil

50ml (2fl oz) white wine vinegar

4 carrots, sliced in two lengthways

2 celery sticks, sliced in three widthways

4 garlic cloves, skins left on

3 sprigs of rosemary

Apricot stuffing

2 garlic cloves, finely chopped

1 bay leaf, crushed by hand

250g (9oz) dried apricots

1 bunch of sage, leaves only

Dry rub

1 tsp dried chilli flakes

1 tbsp fennel seeds, lightly toasted in a dry frying pan and crushed

I've rolled the pork around apricots as I think it's a match made in heaven and a refreshing change from the time-honoured pork–apple partnership, but there's nothing to stop you using another dried fruit, such as prunes.

Preheat the oven to 220°C/425°F/gas mark 7.

Lay the pork loin, meat side down, on a chopping board. With a very sharp knife, score the surface of the skin in diagonal lines at intervals of 1cm (½in). Mix together all the ingredients for the dry rub. Spread over the pork skin, pressing well into the slits. Turn the pork over and season with the sea salt.

To make the stuffing, heat 1 tbsp of the olive oil in a small frying pan over a very low heat and sweat the garlic and bay leaf for 1–2 minutes without browning. Tip the apricots into a food processor with the sage and blitz. Add the garlic and bay leaf and blitz again until the apricots are very finely chopped. Lay the apricot paste in a long even sausage-shape along the length of the loin. Then roll up the pork into a tight roll. Use a sharp knife to trim away any excess belly.

Tie the pork roll with loops of butcher's twine wrapped around the meat at 3cm (1¼in) intervals and tightened with slipknots.

Heat the remaining olive oil in a large roasting tin. Put the pork in the tin, reduce the heat and fry for about 20 minutes, turning the roll to crisp and colour the skin slowly and evenly. To get really crunchy crackling, brush over the vinegar.

Roast the pork for 15 minutes in the hot oven before turning the temperature down to 180°C/350°F/gas mark 4. Remove the roasting tin from the oven, transfer the pork to a plate, and place the carrots, celery, garlic and rosemary in the base of the tin (this layer of veg stops the underneath of the pork from burning). Place the pork on top, then roast for a further 2 hours, turning occasionally, until the centre of the roll reaches 63°C (145°F) (check with a meat thermometer).

Let the meat rest for 20 minutes before carving and serving.

Boned shoulder of pork cooked in milk and peaches

Serves 8

1 tbsp olive oil

100g (3½ oz) butter

1 boned shoulder of pork, skinned and cut into 8 equal pieces

salt and pepper

6 bay leaves

3 garlic cloves, finely sliced

2 onions, finely sliced

1 leek, cleaned, the white end finely sliced, the green end reserved

8 large fresh peaches, stoned and sliced

1 sprig of thyme

1 sprig of rosemary

1 sprig of sage

600ml (1 pint) double cream

2.5 litres (4½ pints) milk

To serve

hunks of bread

steamed green vegetables

I know it sounds weird but this is truly delicious. Trust me: you won't be disappointed. The pork picks up all the flavours, especially that of the peaches, and literally falls off the bone. During the lengthy cooking, the milk, pork fat and peach skins magically combine to form a mouthwatering stock.

Preheat the oven to 150°C/300°F/gas mark 2.

Heat the oil and butter in a very large flameproof casserole or deep roasting tin until the butter is foaming.

Season the pork pieces well and place in the casserole with the bay leaves. Fry and turn until the pork is browned all over. Remove from the casserole and set aside.

Tip the garlic, onions, leek and peaches into the casserole, cover and sweat over a low heat until tender and golden (20–25 minutes).

Return the pork pieces to the casserole. Wrap the herbs in the green leek leaves and tie with a length of butcher's twine. Add to the casserole.

Pour in the cream and half the milk. Bring to a simmer, cover with a lid or kitchen foil and put in the oven to braise for at least 4 hours. Check the level of the liquid regularly and top up with more milk if necessary. By the time the pork is cooked, the sauce should look congealed, because the milk and cream have split.

When the pork is meltingly tender, remove the leek–herb parcel and the bay leaves.

Serve with hunks of bread and steamed green vegetables.

Roast belly of pork with mustard mash and salsa dragoncello

Serves 4

1 pork belly, about 1kg (2lb 4oz), bones and cartilage removed by a butcher

25g (1oz) fennel seeds, lightly toasted in a dry frying pan

1 tsp dried chilli flakes

1 tsp sea salt crystals

1 tbsp olive oil

1 leek, cleaned and roughly chopped

1 carrot, roughly chopped

1 Spanish onion, roughly chopped

Mashed potato

600g (1lb 5oz) floury potatoes (Desiree or Maris Piper), peeled and quartered

100g (3½oz) unsalted butter

1 tbsp wholegrain mustard

1 tbsp extra virgin olive oil

salt and pepper

Salsa dragoncello

½ ciabatta loaf, crusts removed and cut into small cubes

125ml (4fl oz) red wine vinegar

2 hard-boiled free-range egg yolks, mashed with a fork

50g (1¾ oz) capers, finely chopped

10 anchovy fillets, chopped

1 bunch of tarragon, leaves only, chopped

100ml (3½ fl oz) extra virgin olive oil

salt and pepper

In my opinion, belly of pork is the finest cut of pork: bursting with flavour and incredibly succulent. It's important to cook it properly to melt all the fat and keep that to-die-for porkiness.

Preheat the oven to 200°C/400°F/gas mark 6.

Use a sharp knife to score parallel cuts in the skin, 1cm (½in) apart, down the length of the pork belly. Pound the fennel seeds, chilli flakes and sea salt to a powder in a pestle and mortar. Rub all over the pork belly with the olive oil.

Heat a baking sheet over a medium–high heat and lay the belly, skin side down, on top. Fry for 2 minutes, reduce the heat and fry for a further 10 minutes. Remove the pork and set aside.

Spread the vegetables over the bottom of the baking sheet and place the belly, skin upwards, on top. Roast for 30 minutes.

Make the salsa. Soak the bread in the vinegar for 20 minutes. Combine the egg yolks with the capers, anchovies, tarragon, extra virgin olive oil and seasoning. When the bread is soggy, drain off any surplus vinegar into a bowl – squeeze the bread if necessary to get at least 3 tbsp. Chop up the bread and stir into the other salsa ingredients. Set aside in a refrigerator.

After 30 minutes of roasting, turn the oven down to 180°C/350°F/gas mark 4 and pour the 3 tbsp of vinegar over the pork skin. Return to the oven until tender (another 1½ hours).

With 30 minutes of roasting to go, place the potatoes in a saucepan of salted cold water. Bring to the boil, then reduce the heat and boil until tender (15–20 minutes). Drain and return to a low heat for 2–3 minutes, stirring, until any residual water has evaporated. Add the butter, mustard, olive oil and seasoning. Mash until the potatoes are smooth and creamy.

Remove the pork from the oven, cover with kitchen foil and leave to rest for 15 minutes. Divide the mash between 4 plates and arrange thick slices of the pork belly on top. Serve with a dollop of the dragoncello dressing spooned over the meat.

Cheeky-chop sandwich filled with spinach and ricotta with cinnamon roasted apples

Serves 4

4 pork loin chops, about
300–350g (10½–12oz) each

salt and pepper

1 red chilli, deseeded and
finely chopped

2 garlic cloves, finely chopped

1 bunch of fresh sage, leaves only,
finely chopped

150g (5½oz) ricotta cheese,
drained and crumbled

300g (10½oz) leaf spinach,
thick stalks trimmed after
weighing, washed

50ml (2fl oz) olive oil

250ml (9fl oz) white wine

100g (3½oz) butter

100g (3½oz) demerara sugar

4 Cox's apples, cored and put
into cold water with the juice
of 1 lemon

2 tsp ground cinnamon

2 sprigs of rosemary

3 sprigs of thyme

3 bay leaves

Cooking this was the first time I realized that you can do so much more than just fry a chop. I called it Cheeky-chop sandwich because the Fifteen Foundation was originally called *Cheeky Chops* and I cooked it for an assessment there.

Preheat the oven to 200°C/400°F/gas mark 6.

Using a sharp knife, cut horizontally through the middle of the meat, right to the bone, to butterfly the chops. Open out the 2 flaps of each chop like a book. Season and set aside.

Mix half the chilli, garlic and sage into the ricotta in a bowl and season. Cover a small baking sheet with baking paper and spread the ricotta on top. Put in the oven until lightly browned and slightly crusty (10–15 minutes). Set aside.

Heat a large stainless steel saucepan over a medium heat. Tip in the damp spinach and steam briefly before adding 1 tbsp of the oil with the remaining chilli and garlic. Stir-fry briefly before pouring in the wine. Simmer over a low heat for 2–3 minutes until the wine has nearly evaporated. Set aside.

Melt the butter and sugar in an ovenproof frying pan. Add the apples and fry, turning frequently, until the sugar starts to caramelize (about 10 minutes). Roast in the oven until just tender and well coloured (10–15 minutes). Remove from the oven, sprinkle the cinnamon over the top and set aside.

Meanwhile, drain the spinach and season lightly. Tip the spinach and ricotta into a food processor and blitz briefly until well mixed. To stuff the pork chops, spread a quarter of the spinach-ricotta mixture on 1 flap and fold over the other.

Heat the remaining oil in a frying pan. Fry the chops in batches until browned (about 3 minutes each side). Transfer to a roasting sheet, scatter over the remaining sage, the rosemary, thyme and bay leaves, and roast until cooked through (10–12 minutes). Add the apples to the roasting tray for the last 5 minutes. Remove the chops from the oven and leave to rest for 5 minutes before serving with the cinnamon roasted apples.

Pork stew with spicy Italian sausage

Serves 6

3 tbsp olive oil

2 onions, finely chopped

1 celery stick, finely diced

1 carrot, peeled and finely diced

salt and pepper

1 Salsicca (spicy Italian sausage), finely diced

1kg (2lb 4oz) pork shoulder, boned and diced into 2.5cm (1in) pieces

2 tbsp plain flour

1 litre (1¾ pints) hot chicken stock

4 medium Maris Piper potatoes, diced

1 bunch of sage, tied with butcher's twine

To serve

hunks of bread

extra virgin olive oil for drizzling

Humble stews are perfect winter warmers. I personally like this one because there's a hint of Irish influence in it: it reminds me of my mum, who is Irish and makes wonderful stews and casseroles. Filled with fennel seeds, chilli and garlic, the sausages add a very special smoky flavour.

Heat 1 tbsp of the olive oil in a heavy-based saucepan. Add the onions, celery, carrot and salt and pepper. Cover with a lid and sweat over a low heat, checking every 10 minutes until the vegetables are very soft. Remove from the saucepan and set aside.

Raise the heat to medium–high and quickly fry the cubes of sausage in the saucepan until browned all over. (Frying the sausages briefly stops them drying out and becoming chewy.) Remove from the saucepan and set aside. Drain off the fat.

Toss the pieces of pork in the plain flour to give each piece a light dusting. Add 1 tbsp of the olive oil to the same saucepan and place over a medium heat to brown the pork. You may need to fry the pork in two batches to make sure that all the cubes get evenly browned. After removing the first batch from the saucepan, remember to add the remaining olive oil and reheat before frying the second batch. Lift the pork out of the saucepan with a slotted spoon and set aside.

Deglaze the saucepan with the hot chicken stock. Return the pork, sausage and vegetables to the saucepan and add the potatoes and sage. Cover the saucepan with a lid and stew very gently over a low heat for 1½ hours.

Check the pork stew is not getting too dry and cook on, uncovered, until the meat is very tender and the sauce has reduced and thickened (a further 30 minutes).

Remove the sage before serving the pork stew with hunks of bread and drizzles of extra virgin olive oil.

T-bone Florentine

Serves 2

2 T-bone steaks, about 425g (15oz) each, from any good butcher, at room temperature

salt and pepper

1 tbsp olive oil

2 sprigs of rosemary, leaves only

2 garlic cloves, finely chopped

20g (¾oz) unsalted butter

125ml (4fl oz) white wine

Sautéed potatoes

3 large Maris Piper potatoes, peeled and cut into 2cm (¾in) cubes

2 tsp extra virgin olive oil

20g (¾oz) unsalted butter

2 sprigs of rosemary, leaves only

They serve this dish as *Bistecca Fiorentina* at my favourite restaurant in London, *La Famiglia*. Such a superb cut of beef, treated so simply, is absolutely irresistible. You get the best of both worlds: steak as tender as fillet and as tasty as sirloin.

Season the steaks and rub with the oil, rosemary and garlic.

Put the potatoes in a saucepan of lightly salted cold water and bring to the boil. Cook until the cubes are just starting to break up (no more than 10 minutes). Drain immediately. Spread out on a baking sheet and cool as quickly as possible.

Heat 2 heavy-based frying pans large enough to hold a steak. Place a steak in each and fry for 3–7 minutes, depending on the thickness of the steaks, then turn the steaks over and fry for a further 3–7 minutes for rare meat. (For better done meat, cook for 2–3 minutes longer on each side.)

Toss half the butter and wine into each frying pan. Give each frying pan a good shake and take off the heat. Cover the steaks with kitchen foil and set aside in a warm place to rest.

To sauté the potatoes, heat the extra virgin olive oil in another frying pan. Add the potato cubes and sauté (move around the pan while frying) until starting to brown. Throw in the butter and rosemary and continue to sauté until all the potato cubes are crisp and golden brown. Remove from the heat and drain on a sheet of kitchen paper.

Serve the steaks immediately, drizzled with the pan juices, accompanied by the sautéed potatoes.

Slow-braised shin of beef in red wine with oozy polenta and mustard fruits

Serves 6

2 shins of beef on the bone, about 1kg (2lb 4oz) each

1 cinnamon stick

3 star anise

5 bay leaves

8 juniper berries

1 tbsp fennel seeds

1 tbsp mustard seeds

1 tbsp coriander seeds

2 garlic bulbs, cut in half around the middle

2 celery sticks, thinly sliced

2 onions, thinly sliced

2 leeks, cleaned and thinly sliced

2 carrots, thinly sliced

2 bottles of red wine (the Nebbiolo grape is best for this dish)

salt and pepper

50g (1¾ oz) plain flour for dusting

4 tbsp extra virgin olive oil

2 tbsp tomato purée

1 litre (1¾ pints) hot beef or chicken stock

50g (1¾ oz) Mostarda di Cremona (candied fruits spiced with mustard oil available from some Italian delis), to serve (optional)

6 sprigs of thyme, to garnish

Oozy polenta

100g (3½ oz) unsalted butter

375g (13oz) quick-cook polenta

1.4 litres (2½ pints) chicken stock

100g (3½ oz) Parmesan cheese, finely grated

It's a great shame that shin of beef rarely gets used nowadays. So it needs long slow cooking to tenderize it? Okay! But it's well worth the wait: the meat and the marrowbone really deliver loads of satisfying flavour and goodness.

Start preparation 1 or 2 days before you intend to serve this dish. Put the beef in a large, non-metallic ovenproof roasting dish. Lightly crush the spices and bay leaves, tip into the centre of a square of muslin and tie with string. Add to the beef with the garlic and half the celery, onions, leeks and carrots. Pour over the wine, cover with clingfilm and leave to marinate in the refrigerator for at least 24 hours; 48 hours are better still. Turn the meat over in the marinade at halftime.

Preheat the oven to 180°C/350°F/gas mark 4. Remove the meat from the marinade, saving that for later, and dry with kitchen paper. Season and dust with a little flour.

Heat 2 tbsp of olive oil in a large frying pan and brown the shins all over. Heat the remaining olive oil in a roasting tin and add the remaining vegetables. Sweat over a low heat for 5–8 minutes. Stir in the tomato purée and cook for 2–3 minutes. Add the shins with the marinade and spice bag, bring to a simmer and add half the stock. Cover and braise in the oven until the meat is falling off the bone (at least 4 hours). Top up the liquid with the remaining stock or water during cooking. Turn the meat over at halftime.

Place the shins on a plate and set aside. Sieve the stock into a saucepan. Discard the spice bag and press the vegetables through the sieve with the back of a spoon. Stir and season.

For the oozy polenta, melt the butter in a frying pan. Pour in the polenta and stir. Slowly add three-quarters of the stock while stirring briskly over a high heat. Reduce the heat to low and cook for 5 minutes, stirring occasionally. Whisk in the Parmesan with the remaining stock and season to taste.

Strip the meat from the shin bones and reheat in the sauce. Serve with the polenta, and Mostarda di Cremona, if you like. Garnish with sprigs of thyme.

Pan-fried fillet of beef with roasted summer vegetables and freshly grated horseradish

Serves 4

4 barrel fillet steaks,
about 225g (8oz) each

salt and pepper

1 tsp olive oil

4 banana shallots, cut in half

100g (3½oz) butter

Roasted summer vegetables

6 raw baby beetroot

juice and rind of 1 unwaxed lemon

3 bay leaves

2 large red peppers

1 tbsp red wine vinegar

2 tbsp extra virgin olive oil

4 tbsp olive oil

10 Charlotte potatoes, cut into
5mm (½in) wedges

4 garlic cloves, 2 smashed in their
skins, 2 peeled and crushed

1 small bunch of thyme, leaves only

12 pomodorino tomatoes,
dunked in boiling water for
3 seconds and skinned

2 courgettes, halved lengthways,
deseeded with a teaspoon and cut
diagonally into 3cm (1¼in) slices

½ red chilli

250ml (9fl oz) white wine

1 handful of mint leaves, chopped

75ml (2½fl oz) balsamic vinegar,
plus extra for drizzling

3 sprigs of oregano, leaves only

To serve

50g (1¾oz) horseradish root, peeled

extra virgin olive oil for drizzling

Fillet is the cut of beef that sits against the sirloin. As it doesn't do any work, it's extremely tender. However, it hasn't any fat, so it has less flavour than other cuts. Because of this, its advisable to cook it medium–rare at the most. Serve with summer vegetables for loads of texture and sweet flavours.

Preheat the oven to 230°C/450°F/gas mark 8.

Take the fillet steaks out of the refrigerator and place on a chopping board. Season all over and rub in a little olive oil. Set aside to come to room temperature.

Place the beetroot in a flameproof baking dish just large enough hold them all. Half-fill the dish with water and add the lemon rind and bay leaves. Bring to a simmer on top of the stove, cover with a lid or kitchen foil and cook for 30–40 minutes, depending on size.

Meanwhile, to skin the red peppers, hold in the flames of a gas ring or put under a very hot grill until blackened. Transfer the charred peppers to a bowl, cover with clingfilm and leave to sweat. When cool enough to handle comfortably, carefully peel off the charred skins. Cut the skinned peppers in half, remove the seeds and core and tear the flesh into strips. Toss with a little seasoning, the red wine vinegar and 1 tbsp of the extra virgin olive oil and set aside.

Heat 2 tbsp of the olive oil in an ovenproof frying pan or small roasting tin over a high heat. Carefully tip in the potatoes and move them around using a wooden spatula. When the wedges are starting to brown, throw in the smashed garlic and thyme, sprinkle with salt and pepper, transfer to the oven and roast for about 20 minutes.

Crush the pomodorino tomatoes with a fork in a bowl, season with a little salt and pepper and set aside.

Heat the remaining olive oil in a sauté pan and fry the courgettes until lightly browned all over. Stir in the crushed garlic and the chilli and fry for 30 seconds without burning

the garlic. Deglaze the pan with half of the wine and simmer to reduce. Remove from the heat, stir in the mint while still hot and set aside.

Heat a large ovenproof frying pan over a high heat and arrange the steaks well apart from each other. Brown the meat on both sides and add the shallots. Throw in 55g (2oz) of the butter and colour the steaks and shallots all over. Transfer to a plate and pour off the pan juices into a small bowl and set aside. Return the steaks to the frying pan and roast in the oven for about 6 minutes for rare, 8 minutes for medium–rare. (Never cook fillet steak more than medium–rare as it dries out easily.)

Take the potato wedges out of the oven and keep warm.

Drain the beetroot, slide off the skins and cut in half. Put in a bowl and add the balsamic vinegar, lemon juice and a sprinkling of oregano leaves. Season and set aside in a warm place.

Take the steaks out of the oven and turn them over. Cover with kitchen foil and rest in a warm place for 5 minutes.

While the steaks are resting, put the beetroot, red peppers courgettes and potato wedges in the oven to reheat.

Remove the steaks from the pan and return the shallots to the heat with the remaining butter and the pan juices set aside earlier. Scrape any residue from the bottom of the pan and deglaze with the remaining wine. Reduce quickly over a high heat to make a sauce.

Share out the roasted vegetables between 4 hot plates. Cut the rested fillets in half horizontally and arrange on the vegetables. Spoon the shallots and a little sauce around the plate. Grate some fresh horseradish over the top and drizzle with the balsamic vinegar and extra virgin olive oil.

Pan-fried calves' livers with olive-oil mash, balsamic figs and crisp pancetta

Serves 4

675g (1lb 8oz) trimmed calves'
livers, thinly sliced

8 thin slices pancetta

50g (1¾oz) unsalted butter

1 bunch of sage, leaves only

Balsamic figs

50g (1¾oz) unsalted butter

4 large ripe black figs, stalks
removed and cut into quarters

3 tbsp balsamic vinegar

salt and pepper

Olive-oil mash

1kg (2lb 4oz) Maris Piper potatoes,
peeled and quartered

50ml (2fl oz) extra virgin olive oil

25g (1oz) unsalted butter

salt

When I was a kid, my mum used to cook liver and bacon for dinner and I hated it – well, I loathed most food when I was a kid but liver was my pet hate. But since I've become a chef my taste buds have changed. Now I think liver tastes marvellous with balsamic vinegar and pancetta.

To prepare the olive-oil mash, put the potatoes in a large saucepan of lightly salted cold water and bring to the boil. Simmer until cooked.

Meanwhile, take the liver out of the refrigerator, season well on both sides and allow to come to room temperature.

To cook the balsamic figs, melt the butter in a frying pan and fry the figs for 5 minutes over a high heat. Pour in the balsamic vinegar, turn the heat down low and let the figs stew for a further 10 minutes. Season with salt and pepper.

Lay the slices of pancetta on a grill tray and position as far down as possible under a grill on a low heat to crisp up slowly without burning. For extra crispness, turn the slices over during grilling.

When the potatoes are cooked, drain off the water. Return the saucepan to a low heat and stir the potatoes around with a wooden spoon until any residual water has evaporated. Pour in the olive oil, add the butter and beat vigorously with the wooden spoon until thoroughly blended and smooth. Season to taste with the salt and set aside in a warm place.

To fry the liver, heat the butter in 2 large nonstick frying pans. When foaming, add the liver and sage to the pans. Fry for 2 minutes until the liver is well browned on the underside. Turn the slices over and fry for a further 2 minutes. Stir in the balsamic figs and remove from the heat.

To serve, spoon a mound of mashed potatoes into the centre of each plate and arrange the liver on top. Place the figs over and around the liver and drizzle on the sauce. Top off each serving with 2 slices of crisp pancetta.

Easter leg of kid with cipollini onions and mint

I don't know why goat isn't more popular because it's got a lot going for it. It's low in cholesterol, which makes it one of the healthiest meats, and it's cheap. It also roasts and stews beautifully. The meat tastes a bit more gamey than lamb, and may be a little tougher, but it's just as delicious. You won't find it in many supermarkets but you should be able to order it from any good butcher.

Serves 4

800g (1lb 12oz) new potatoes, cut in half

500g (1lb 2oz) carrots, cut into batons

400g (14oz) cipollini (baby onions)

1 leg of kid (baby goat), about 1kg (2lb 4oz)

salt and pepper

5 sprigs of rosemary

3 garlic cloves, cut in half

6 tbsp olive oil, plus extra for drizzling

1 bunch of sage, leaves only

3 bay leaves

1 bunch of flat leaf parsley, leaves only, chopped

1 bunch of fresh mint leaves, leaves only, chopped

Put the potatoes, carrots and cipollini in a saucepan of lightly salted boiling water and cook for about 6 minutes. Drain and set aside.

Preheat the oven to 180°C/350°F/gas mark 4.

Place the leg of kid in a roasting tin and season with salt and pepper. Smash 3 sprigs of the rosemary and the garlic in a pestle and mortar, then add the oil. Rub the herb oil vigorously over the leg of kid.

Add the drained vegetables to the roasting tin and roast for about 1¼ hours. After 30 minutes of roasting, add the remaining rosemary, the sage and bay leaves, drizzle with some olive oil and stir before returning to the oven.

When cooked, turn off the oven. Remove the meat and set aside to rest for 10 minutes but leave the vegetables in to keep warm. Tear the meat from the bone and sprinkle with the parsley and fresh mint. To serve, divide the meat and roasted vegetables between 4 plates and pour over any meat juices from the roasting tin.

Roman spring lamb casserole

Serves 4

4 medium potatoes, peeled and cut into 3mm (⅛ in) slices

1 leg of spring lamb, about 1kg (2lb 4oz), boned and diced into 2.5cm (1in) pieces

plain flour for dusting

3 tbsp olive oil

salt and pepper

6 sprigs of rosemary, leaves only

1 bunch of sage, leaves only, chopped

4 garlic cloves, coarsely chopped

175ml (6fl oz) fruity red wine

6 tbsp red wine vinegar

850ml (1½ pints) brown meat stock

1 tbsp extra virgin olive oil

50g (1¾oz) butter

steamed spinach, to serve

Apparently Roman army cooks would chuck all the ingredients for a nourishing stew like this into a large caldron and leave it simmering over the campfire while the soldiers went off to fight a battle. Any weary survivors who made it back to camp would be rewarded with a warming feast.

Put the potatoes in a saucepan of lightly salted cold water and bring to the boil. Cook until nearly tender (8–10 minutes). Drain and set aside.

Preheat the oven to 180°C/350°F/gas mark 4.

Toss the lamb in the plain flour to give each piece a light dusting. Heat the olive oil in a large, deep roasting tin, add the lamb and cook over a high heat, turning frequently, until browned all over.

Season with salt and pepper then sprinkle over the rosemary, sage and garlic. Shake the tin to mix up the flavours.

Stir in the red wine and red wine vinegar and boil until the liquid has almost evaporated.

Add enough meat stock to cover the lamb, then top up with 2cm (¾in) more. Layer the parboiled potatoes on top, drizzle with the extra virgin olive oil and dot the butter all over. Cover with kitchen foil and cook in the oven until the meat is tender (30–45 minutes). Add a little more stock if the casserole seems to be drying out. Remove the foil for the last 15 minutes of cooking to brown the potatoes.

Serve with some steamed spinach.

Slow-roasted shoulder of lamb with spring greens in an anchovy and rosemary dressing

Serves 5–6

1 shoulder of lamb, about
1.8kg (4lb)

salt and pepper

1 bulb of garlic, cut in half
around the middle

2 sprigs of rosemary

juice and rind of 1 unwaxed lemon

2 tbsp olive oil

1 carrot, chopped

1 celery stick, chopped

1 Spanish onion, cut into 8 wedges

Spring greens

4 anchovy fillets, finely chopped

1 sprig of rosemary, leaves only,
finely chopped

2 tbsp extra virgin olive oil

2 heads of spring greens, stems
removed, leaves shredded into
3cm (1¼ in) strips

salt and pepper

After slow-roasting, spring lamb is wondrously tender and tasty: the melting fat has a chance to seep through the meat, carrying with it masses of flavour and succulence. Serving the lamb with spring greens in an anchovy and rosemary dressing lifts the whole dish to new heights of deliciousness.

Use a sharp knife to score a cross-hatched pattern of 2.5cm (1in) squares across the skin of the lamb. Rub the shoulder all over with salt, pepper, garlic, rosemary, lemon rind and olive oil. For greater flavour, set aside to marinate in the refrigerator overnight.

Preheat the oven to 230°C/450°F/gas mark 8.

Heat a large heavy-based frying pan. When hot, fry the skin side of the shoulder until evenly browned.

Put the vegetables, garlic, rosemary and lemon peel in a roasting tin and lay the lamb on top. Roast for 20 minutes, then reduce the temperature to 180°C/350°F/gas mark 4. Cover the tin loosely with kitchen foil and roast for a further 4 hours, basting frequently, until the meat is practically falling off the bone.

Meanwhile, mix the anchovies, rosemary, lemon juice and extra virgin olive oil together. Set aside in the refrigerator.

When the lamb is cooked, bring a saucepan of lightly salted water to the boil. Cook the greens for 4–5 minutes, drain into a colander and return to the saucepan. Stir in the anchovy and rosemary dressing and season well with salt and pepper.

Tear the lamb off the bone and serve with the hot spring greens and the meat juices from the roasting tin.

Polenta-crusted rack of lamb with potato and artichoke al forno

Serves 2

2 tsp Dijon mustard

1 rack of lamb (7 best-end cutlets), skinned, trimmed and chined (spinal bones removed) by a butcher

40g (1½oz) polenta

salt and pepper

Potato and artichoke *al forno*

50g (1¾oz) butter

450g (1lb) waxy potatoes (Charlotte, Roosevelt or Anya), cut into 5mm (½in) slices

salt and pepper

5 sprigs of lemon thyme, leaves only

4 globe artichokes, trimmed, petals and chokes removed, hearts sliced into cold water with the juice of 1 lemon

100ml (3½fl oz) double cream

50g (1¾oz) Parmesan, finely grated

To serve

rocket leaves (optional)

extra virgin olive oil for drizzling

This is an ace partnership: when you bite into the lamb, the crunchy polenta crust hits you as an amazing contrast to the tender meat. I've found that the rack is best roasted at an even oven temperature rather than grilled or barbecued, where the polenta can easily get scorched. The potatoes and artichokes simply make a nice moist accompaniment.

Preheat the oven to 220°C/425°F/gas mark 7.

Spread the mustard all over the rack of lamb. Sprinkle the polenta and some seasoning on to a baking sheet. Roll the meat through the grains to coat evenly and set aside.

For the potato and artichoke *al forno*, butter a small baking dish and arrange a layer of potato slices in the base. Season with salt and pepper and a sprinkling of thyme leaves. Top with a layer of drained artichoke slices, then another of potato, seasoning each layer, until all the potato and artichoke have been used, finishing with a layer of potato. Pour over the double cream and sprinkle with the grated Parmesan.

Cover with kitchen foil and bake for 25 minutes. Remove the foil and continue baking for a further 25 minutes until the top has browned.

Meanwhile, place the rack of lamb, bone side down, in a roasting tin lined with baking paper. Roast for 25 minutes for pink meat, 35 minutes for better done. Transfer the lamb to a carving board and leave to rest for 5 minutes in a warm place.

To serve, place a large spoonful of the potato and artichoke *al forno* in the centre of each plate. Lay a few rocket leaves over the potato, if you like. Carve the rack of lamb into cutlets and arrange on top. Finish with a drizzle of extra virgin olive oil.

Spatchcocked poussin with beetroot, spring greens and herb mascarpone

Serves 4

4 poussins (whole young chickens), back bones removed and whole birds flattened (spatchcocked)

salt and pepper

3 tbsp olive oil

50g (1¾oz) butter

500ml (18fl oz) white wine

250g (9oz) mascarpone cheese

1 small bunch each of basil, mint and flat leaf parsley, coarsely chopped

Beetroot and spring greens

4 large raw beetroots, about 600g (1lb 5oz) in total, washed

1 bunch of thyme

juice and rind of 1 unwaxed lemon

1 head of spring greens, stems removed and leaves shredded

1 tbsp olive oil

1 tsp chopped garlic

1 tsp chopped red chilli

1 tbsp balsamic vinegar

1 tbsp extra virgin olive oil

salt and pepper

In Italy, the technique of roasting under a brick is known as *al mattone*. Not only does pressing the spatchcocked poussins to the pan guarantee a golden, crisp skin but also ensures that the breasts and legs cook in the same time and stay moist.

Preheat the oven to 220°C/425°F/gas mark 7. Bring a saucepan of lightly salted cold water to the boil.

Place the beetroot in a roasting tin with the thyme and lemon rind and pour in enough hot water to half-fill the tin. Cover with kitchen foil and poach until the beetroot are soft enough to insert a knife easily (50–60 minutes).

Meanwhile, season the poussins and rub 2 tbsp of the olive oil into the skins. Heat another tbsp of the olive oil in a large, heavy-based frying pan over a high heat. Put the poussins, 2 at a time, skin side down, in the pan. Place another frying pan on top and weigh the poussins down with a foil-wrapped brick. Reduce the heat to medium to avoid burning the skin. Fry until the skins are golden brown (5–6 minutes). Transfer to a roasting tin, skin side up, and repeat with the other 2 poussins. Roast alongside the beetroot until cooked through (15–20 minutes).

Meanwhile, blanch the spring greens in salted boiling water for 5 minutes and drain. Heat the olive oil in a saucepan, add the greens with the garlic and chilli and stir-fry for 1–2 minutes.

Remove the beetroot from the oven and set aside until cool enough to handle. Rub off the skins and cut into chunky wedges. Transfer to a bowl and pour over the lemon juice, balsamic vinegar and extra virgin olive oil. Season to taste.

Remove the poussins from the roasting tin and set aside. Put the roasting tin on the hob and add the butter. Deglaze with the wine and boil fiercely for 3–4 minutes to reduce and thicken.

Mix the mascarpone and herbs together and stir into the roasting tin. Adjust the seasoning to taste. Pour the sauce into a jug. Serve the poussins on a bed of beetroot wedges and spring greens with the mascarpone herb sauce poured over the top.

Roasted duck breast in holy-wine sauce with pomegranate seeds

Serves 4

4 Gressingham or Barbary duck breasts, about 225g (8oz) each, trimmed of sinew and excess fat

salt and pepper

100g (3½oz) unsalted butter

100ml (3½ fl oz) Vin Santo (holy wine)

seeds from 1 large pomegranate

2 tbsp extra virgin olive oil for drizzling

When you cook a duck breast, always remember to score the skin and start cooking it with the skin side down in a cold pan over a medium heat. This way, the fat has time to heat up and melt evenly without burning the skin. As luck would have it, duck and parsnips are in season at the same time and go very well together (*see* page 94).

Remove the duck breasts from the refrigerator and set aside on a chopping board to come to room temperature. Score the skin in a criss-cross pattern with a sharp knife. Rub salt and pepper over the skin and meat.

Preheat the oven to 230°C/450°F/gas mark 8.

Lay the duck breasts, skin side down, into a cold large heavy-based frying pan and place over a medium–high heat. After 3–4 minutes, as the fat is starting to melt, turn the heat down to low–medium and continue frying until the skin is browned and crisp.

Flip the breasts over on to a baking sheet and put in the oven to roast until well browned, firm and cooked through (7–9 minutes). Transfer the breasts to a carving board and cover with kitchen foil.

Melt the butter in a frying pan with salt and pepper. When bubbling, deglaze the pan with the Vin Santo. Simmer for 2–3 minutes before throwing in 4 handfuls of pomegranate seeds. Heat through and set the sauce aside.

Cut each breast into 5 slices with a sharp knife and serve immediately with the sauce and pomegranate seeds poured over the top and a drizzle of extra virgin olive oil.

Pot-roasted pheasant with mixed fruits

Serves 2

1 pheasant, plucked and drawn

1 tbsp olive oil

salt and pepper

1 clementine

50g (1¾oz) streaky bacon

20g (¾oz) unsalted butter

2 Williams pears, peeled

1 punnet of blackberries

4 black figs, stalks removed and cut into quarters

2 bay leaves

4 juniper berries, crushed

1 tbsp redcurrant jelly

1 tbsp port wine

Bruschetta

1 ciabatta loaf, thickly sliced

1 garlic clove, cut in half

1 tbsp extra virgin olive oil

Take my word for it: pot-roasted pheasant is outstanding when made with fresh birds in the autumn. I think the warm fragrant fruits are a delightful combination too: both with themselves and with the pheasant. Try serving this dish with some oozy polenta (see page 78).

Preheat the oven to 140°C/275°F/gas mark 1.

Rinse out the body cavity of the pheasant. Rub the skin with olive oil and season all over. Push the clementine into the cavity and wrap the streaky bacon around the breasts. Tie the rashers in place with some butcher's twine.

Melt the butter in a frying pan and fry the pheasant, lying on one leg, for 3–4 minutes, before turning the bird over on to the other leg and frying for a further 3–4 minutes.

Sit the whole pears in a deep ovenproof dish with a lid. Add the blackberries, black figs, bay leaves and juniper berries. Pour about 5mm (½in) of water into the bottom of the dish and nestle the pheasant among the fruit. Braise in the oven for 1½ hours, until cooked through, basting frequently to keep the breasts moist.

Transfer the bird to a carving board, cover with kitchen foil and set aside to rest for 10 minutes.

Pass the cooking juices through a sieve into a small saucepan and set aside the fruit. To make a fruity sauce, add the redcurrant jelly and port to the saucepan. Bring to the boil and simmer to reduce and slightly thicken the sauce (3–4 minutes).

Meanwhile, to prepare the bruschetta, brush each slice of ciabatta with the olive oil. Toast on a griddle pan until crisp with clear bar marks. Rub the cut face of the garlic over each slice of ciabatta.

Serve a leg and a breast per portion, arranged on the bruschetta. Divide the fruit between the 2 plates and drizzle the sauce over the top.

Confit of rabbit with honey-roasted parsnips

Serves 4

8 rabbit legs

25g (1oz) sel gris (moist French sea salt) or rock salt

2 sprigs of thyme

2 sprigs of rosemary

2 juniper berries, crushed

2 tsp coriander seeds

2 tsp mustard seeds

3 garlic cloves, crushed

3 bay leaves

2 black peppercorns, cracked

750g (1lb 10oz) duck fat

Honey-roasted parsnips

600g (1lb 5oz) parsnips, peeled and quartered

600ml (1 pint) semi-skimmed milk (optional)

salt and cracked black pepper

1 tbsp clear honey

2 sprigs of rosemary, leaves only

100g (3½oz) butter

This is a brilliant way to cook rabbit: all the herbs and spices enhance the flavour of the leg meat while the slow cooking at a low temperature tenderizes and moistens it. By the time the confit is ready to eat, the humble rabbit has been transformed into a meltingly tender, aromatic meal.

To give the rabbit time to marinate, you have to start preparing this recipe at least 12 hours before you want to serve it. Lay the rabbit legs on a bed of salt, herbs, berries, spices and garlic, all mixed together well, and set aside to marinate in the refrigerator for 12 hours or overnight. Turn the rabbit legs over occasionally.

Next day, remove the rabbit from the refrigerator and set aside for 30 minutes to reach room temperature.

Preheat the oven to 150°C/300°F/gas mark 2. Wash the salt and spices off the legs and dry thoroughly with kitchen paper. Melt the duck fat in a large, deep, heavy-based ovenproof saucepan and lower the rabbit legs in gently.

Place the saucepan in the oven until the meat is soft and tender (about 3 hours). Set aside to cool a little before pouring the contents of the pan into a container. Put the confit in the refrigerator. (Chilled and stored in a sterile container, confit meat keeps well for a month.)

Turn the oven up to 220°C/425°F/gas mark 7.

Meanwhile, put the parsnip quarters in a large saucepan with the milk or cold water, add a pinch of salt and bring to a simmer. Immediately drain the parsnips and set aside to cool.

Brown the cooked rabbit legs for 2–3 minutes in an ovenproof frying pan, then roast until crisp (10–15 minutes).

While the rabbit is roasting, put the parsnips in a roasting tin, drizzle with honey, sprinkle with the pepper and rosemary and dot with the butter. Roast for 7–8 minutes until coloured.

Serve 2 rabbit legs per portion, each with a bundle of honey-roasted parsnips.

Chicken liver pâté with fig chutney and lavosh

Serves 6

Chicken liver pâté

2 tbsp olive oil

85g (3oz) anchovy fillets

1 banana shallot, finely chopped

450g (1lb) chicken livers, trimmed of sinew and green patches

salt and pepper

50g (1¾oz) unsalted butter

100g (3½oz) baby capers

1 tbsp Vin Santo

1 tbsp port wine

100ml (3½ fl oz) clarified butter (the clear golden liquid part of melted butter)

Fig chutney

200g (7oz) dried figs, topped and chopped

100ml (3½ fl oz) hot water

1 cinnamon stick

1 star anise

2 bay leaves

25g (1oz) caster sugar

20g (¾oz) butter

1 red onion, finely chopped

1 apple (Cox's or Pink Lady), peeled, cored and finely chopped

2 tbsp port wine

2 tsp red wine vinegar

2 tbsp balsamic vinegar

sea salt crystals

Lavosh (see page 187), to serve

This is a great standby to have tucked away in the fridge as an instant snack or starter. Best of all, it's no hassle to make. Neither is the chutney, which is marvellous for livening up a platter of cheeses or antipasti.

To make the chutney, place the chopped figs in a saucepan or heatproof glass bowl with the hot water, spices, bay leaves and sugar and leave to soak for 7–8 minutes until plumped up and softened. Drain any remaining liquid into a small bowl.

Melt the butter in a frying pan and fry the rehydrated figs and spices with the onion and apple over a low heat for 15 minutes, stirring occasionally. Then turn the heat up. When the figs are starting to brown and the frying pan is hot, pour in the port wine. Leave until completely evaporated before adding the red wine vinegar. Again, reduce until the vinegar has evaporated. Finally add the balsamic vinegar and soaking liquid.

Simmer the chutney on a low heat until sticky. Remove the cinnamon stick, star anise and bay leaves and set aside. (If making in advance, store the chutney in a sterilized airtight container until needed.)

To prepare the chicken liver pâté, pour the olive oil into a heavy-based frying pan and sweat the anchovies and shallot together over a low heat until the shallot is softened and the anchovies are starting to break up. Season the livers and add to the frying pan with the butter. Fry for 5 minutes on each side until well browned.

Add the capers and deglaze the frying pan with the Vin Santo and port wine. When the wine has almost evaporated, tip everything into a food processor and blend to a smooth paste. Adjust the seasoning to taste. Pour the pâté into an earthenware or china dish. Smooth the surface and pour on the clarified butter. When cool, place in the refrigerator to firm up.

To serve, put a tbsp of chicken liver pâté on each plate with a neat spoonful of chutney. Garnish with a sprinkling of sea salt and serve with the Lavosh.

Roast venison with juniper gravy

I've learned to treat venison with the respect it deserves. By simply roasting with a few herbs, I make sure that its distinctive flavour is the star of the show. The juniper-scented gravy is there to knock the roughest edges off its gaminess.

Serves 6–8

1 haunch of venison, about 2kg (4lb 8oz), bone removed by a butcher
salt and pepper
6 fresh bay leaves
3 sprigs of thyme
3 sprigs of rosemary
14 rashers of streaky bacon or pancetta
1 tbsp olive oil
100g (3½oz) butter

Juniper gravy
125ml (4fl oz) red wine
300ml (½ pint) meat stock
3 juniper berries, crushed
1 tsp redcurrant jelly (optional)

Preheat the oven to 220°C/425°F/gas mark 7.

Season the venison well with pepper all over and lay the herbs on top of the meat. Drape the bacon over the herbs and hold everything in place with butcher's twine.

Roast the venison parcel in a roasting tin with the olive oil and butter for 20 minutes. Reduce the heat to 170°C/325°F/gas mark 3 and roast for a further 24 minutes per kilo for pink meat, longer for better done. (Alternatively, use a meat thermometer to check how well done the venison is: about 54°C for rare and 59°C for medium–rare.)

When the venison is cooked, transfer the joint to a carving board, cover with foil and set aside to rest in a warm place for at least 20 minutes.

Meanwhile, to make the gravy, deglaze the roasting tin with the wine, scraping any sediment off the base. Pour in the stock, toss in the juniper berries and simmer to reduce and slightly thicken the gravy. Pass through a fine sieve and stir in the redcurrant jelly, if you want to add a little sweetness.

Save the bacon to serve with the venison but discard the herbs. Carve the rested joint and serve the slices with the juniper gravy.

fish &
shellfish

Us Brits don't really prepare or cook fish in our homes as much as our fellow Europeans do, which is a shame as there are many wonderful, flavourful fish available.

When you buy fish, look out for bright red gills; clear, bright, slightly bulging eyes; shiny, tight scales (with none missing); moist, bright skin; and firm flesh.

If you haven't prepared fish before, why not give it a go? First, scale the fish. Hold the fish by the tail and use the back of a sharp knife to scrape towards the head until the flesh is smooth. Second, gut the fish. This is a simple but messy process. Make a slit in the stomach and remove the entrails, then rinse the fish thoroughly under cold running water.

To fillet, use a sharp knife to make an incision just behind the head, then insert the knife under the flesh along the backbone, cutting with clean, sweeping strokes until you release the whole fillet (*see* photos, page 163). Sever the ends of the fillet at the head and tail. Turn the fish over and repeat on the other side.

Finally, pull out the smaller set of bones, called pin bones, that run through the centre of the fillet. Use your finger to feel for the pin bone tips, then use tweezers to pull them out.

Grilled rainbow trout with orange and watercress salad and toasted flaked almonds

This simple dish is typical of the Sicilian culture of cooking excellent street food. I like to eat this fish with a fresh salad and a cold pint of Peroni at a barbecue under a hot sun. For a more dramatic effect, use a special Italian blood orange, which is in season from December to April.

Serves 1

1 whole rainbow trout, about 300g (10½ oz), scaled and gutted
2 tbsp extra virgin olive oil
salt and pepper
2 tbsp flaked almonds, toasted in a dry frying pan until golden
1 orange, peeled and sliced into rings
1 handful of watercress
juice of ½ lemon

Preheat a griddle pan over a high heat.

Use a sharp knife to score the trout with 3 or 4 deep slashes on each side. Drizzle over 1 tbsp of the olive oil, sprinkle with seasoning and rub in well.

Place the trout on the hot griddle for 8 minutes. Then carefully turn it over and repeat on the other side.

Meanwhile, mix the almonds, orange and watercress in a medium bowl. Drizzle over the remaining olive oil and the lemon juice and toss well together. Serve with the rainbow trout.

Grilled salmon with fennel and pine nut salad and zucchini fritti

Serves 4

4 thick salmon fillets, about
175g (6oz) each, pin boned
(fine bones removed with
tweezers) and skinned
salt and pepper
1 tbsp olive oil
1 lemon, cut into wedges

Zucchini fritti

50g (1¾oz) plain flour
50g (1¾oz) rice flour
½ tsp baking powder
salt and pepper
90ml (3fl oz) ice-cold water
1 tsp clear honey
300ml (½ pint) vegetable oil
5 tbsp soda water
4 baby courgettes with flowers
or 2 small courgettes, cut in half
with the seeds scraped out

Fennel and pine nut salad

2 fennel bulbs, outer leaves
removed, tops trimmed (green
fronds saved) and cut in half
100g (3½oz) pine nuts, lightly
toasted in a dry frying pan
½ red chilli, deseeded and
finely chopped
8 sun-blushed tomatoes, chopped
100g (3½oz) crème fraîche
juice and rind of 1 unwaxed lemon
salt and pepper

Here I've come up with a crunchy salad in a creamy dressing that I believe does justice to a gorgeous piece of crispy skinned grilled salmon. Ideally you should buy line-caught salmon, as the quality is out of this world. Otherwise always go for wild salmon.

To make the batter for the *fritti*, tip all the dry ingredients into a bowl and season with salt and pepper. Pour the ice-cold water into a measuring jug and stir in the honey. Whisk the liquid into the flour to make a thick, smooth batter and set aside. (If the batter is very stiff, add a little extra water to loosen it slightly.)

To prepare the salad, finely slice the fennel bulbs on a mandolin or by hand and place in a bowl with the green fennel tops. Mix in the pine nuts, chilli and tomatoes. Stir in the crème fraîche, lemon rind and half the lemon juice. Set aside in a refrigerator.

Pour the vegetable oil into a large, deep saucepan and heat to frying temperature (190°C/375°F), for frying the courgette fritters. Preheat the grill to medium.

Season the salmon well and rub all over with the olive oil. Griddle over a medium heat until firm but still moist (about 8–10 minutes), turning halfway. Pour the remaining lemon juice from the salad over the salmon and set aside to rest.

Gently stir the soda water into the batter. Mix until the batter has the consistency of double cream. It should coat the back of a spoon thickly but pour freely.

Dip the courgettes in the batter and carefully lower into the oil, letting them fall away from you to avoid getting splashed. Fry until golden brown (about 4–5 minutes). Drain on a paper towel and season well with salt.

To serve, divide the salad between 4 plates and place a piece of salmon on top. Arrange the piping hot *fritti* on the side and serve with a wedge of lemon and a twist of black pepper.

Seared swordfish with panzanella salad and tomato oil

Serves 4

4 swordfish steaks, about
300g (10½oz) each

salt and pepper

1 tbsp olive oil

balsamic vinegar for drizzling

Tomato oil

500ml (18fl oz) tomato juice

3 tbsp Tuscan extra virgin olive oil

1 tsp balsamic vinegar

Panzanella salad

600g (1lb 5oz) cherry tomatoes,
cut in half

1 red onion, sliced as thinly
as possible

5 anchovy fillets

4 tbsp capers

1 bunch of basil, leaves only, torn

2 garlic cloves, thinly sliced

4 slices ciabatta bread, about
1cm (½in) thick, toasted and
cut into cubes

1 red chilli, deseeded and sliced
(optional)

2 tbsp red wine vinegar

6 tbsp Tuscan extra virgin olive oil

salt and pepper

I prefer to cook fresh ingredients in season and there are usually plenty of swordfish around at a good price in the summer. This meaty but delicate fish is a star but it needs a few sharp, robust characters on the plate beside it to bring it to life. I've used 'characters' deliberately, because I think it's a bit like casting a film. Here I've chosen tomatoes in the main supporting role with a load of bit parters in the panzanella, and the Italian bubble and squeak, which uses up all the leftovers from the previous night's feast. I think it's got the makings of an Oscar-winning performance.

Remove the swordfish from the refrigerator. Season and rub with olive oil. Set aside to come to room temperature.

To prepare the tomato oil, pour the tomato juice into a saucepan. Bring to the boil over a medium heat and simmer to reduce by half. Set aside to cool. When cool, pour into a mixing bowl with the olive oil and balsamic vinegar and whisk together briskly.

To make the panzanella salad, toss all the ingredients together in a large mixing bowl with your hands. Really squeeze everything together to bring out all the lovely flavours. Divide the salad between 4 plates.

Place the swordfish steaks on a hot griddle or barbecue and cook for 2 minutes on each side for medium rare, longer for better done.

To serve, arrange a swordfish steak on top of the salad and drizzle over tomato oil and balsamic vinegar.

Whole baked seabream with green beans and oregano dressing

Seabream is very similar to seabass, with the same flaky flesh and creamy flavour, but a bit cheaper. It bakes beautifully and needs nothing more than some light seasoning and a few fresh herbs to bring out its best features. I think it goes particularly well with the Shaved fennel, apple and Pecorino Sardo salad (*see* page 171), washed down with a chilled glass of dry white wine. Bring it on!

Serves 4

4 whole seabream, about 300–400g (10½–14oz), scaled and gutted
4 sprigs of basil
1 lemon, quartered
2 tbsp olive oil
50g (1¾oz) unsalted butter
250g (9oz) extra fine green beans, topped and tailed
salt and pepper

Oregano dressing
1 bunch of oregano, leaves only
2 tbsp olive oil
juice of ½ lemon
salt and pepper

Preheat the oven to 200°C/400°F/gas mark 6. Season the fish and stuff the cavities with the basil and lemon quarters.

Heat 1 tbsp of the olive oil and half the butter in each of 2 large nonstick ovenproof frying pans over a medium heat. Put 2 fish in each frying pan and fry until the skin on the underside is browned (about 5 minutes). Turn over and bake in the oven for 15–18 minutes.

To prepare the oregano dressing, mix all the ingredients together.

While the fish is baking, blanch the green beans for 3 minutes in some lightly salted boiling water. Drain and divide the beans between the 2 frying pans with the seabream for the last few minutes of cooking.

Serve the seabream and green beans together, drizzled with the oregano dressing.

Pan-fried seabass supreme with potato and artichoke al forno and olive tapenade

Serves 4

4 seabass supremes (prime pieces of thick fillets), about 175g (6oz) each

2 tbsp olive oil

20g (¾oz) butter, finely diced

Potato and artichoke *al forno*

50g (1¾oz) butter

450g (1lb) waxy potatoes (Charlotte, Rosavelt or Anya), cut into 5mm (½in) slices on a mandolin or by hand

salt and pepper

5 sprigs of lemon thyme, leaves only

2 tbsp extra virgin olive oil

4 globe artichokes, trimmed, chokes removed (*see* page 31) and hearts sliced into cold water with the juice of 1 lemon

Black olive tapenade

100g (3½oz) taggiasca or small black olives, pitted and roughly chopped

1 tbsp finely chopped shallot

2 garlic cloves, chopped

1 tbsp chopped capers

1 red chilli, deseeded and chopped

2 tsp red wine vinegar

1 tbsp chopped celery heart

1 tbsp chopped celery leaves

1 small bunch of flat leaf parsley, finely chopped

200ml (7oz) extra virgin olive oil

Seabass has a creamy, flaky texture, which contrasts brilliantly with its crisply fried skin. The potato and artichoke *al forno* is really delicious but quite rich, so you only need to serve a little with the fish.

Preheat the oven to 220°C/425°F/gas mark 7.

To prepare the *al forno*, butter a small deep baking tray. Arrange a layer of potato in the bottom. Sprinkle with salt, pepper, thyme and a drizzle of olive oil. Top with a layer of drained artichoke slices. Build up layers of potato and artichoke slices, seasoning each layer. Finish with a layer of potato and a drizzle of olive oil.

Cover the top with kitchen foil and bake in the oven for 25 minutes. Remove the foil and bake for a further 5–10 minutes until the top has browned. Turn off the oven but leave the *al forno* inside to keep hot.

Meanwhile, combine all the ingredients for the tapenade in a mixing bowl.

With a sharp knife, slash the skin of the seabass 4 times on each side and rub a little olive oil into the skin. Heat the rest of the olive oil in a heavy-based frying pan until very hot. Then press each fillet firmly on to the base of the frying pan, skin side down. Place another heavy-based frying pan on top to weigh the fish down. Reduce the heat and fry until the underside of the fish is opaque and cooked (about 5 minutes).

Remove the weighting pan, add the butter to the frying pan and turn up the heat slightly to get the butter foaming. Turn over the seabass and fry for a further 2–3 minutes. Set aside in a warm place to finish cooking.

Serve the seabass with the potato and artichoke *al forno* and heaps of black olive tapenade.

Roasted John Dory with lemon thyme, Roosevelt potatoes, taggiasca olives and salsa verde

As far as I'm concerned, John Dory is without a doubt the best meal in the ocean. Although not the best-looking catch on the market, it's definitely the tastiest. Roasted with fragrant lemon thyme, it's sure to win everyone over. Not to worry if you can't get hold of Roosevelt potatoes: after being roasted with extra virgin olive oil and sprinkled with sea salt crystals, any waxy potatoes will be fine.

Serves 2

50g (1¾oz) butter
50ml (2fl oz) olive oil, plus 1 tbsp for frying
300g (10½oz) Roosevelt potatoes, cut into 5mm (½in) slices
1 small bunch of lemon thyme
70g (2½oz) black taggiasca olives, pitted and roughly chopped
salt and pepper
1 whole John Dory, filleted
1 small bunch of tarragon, leaves only

To serve
2 tbsp salsa verde (*see* Barbecued belly pork, page 136)
extra virgin olive oil for drizzling

Preheat the oven to 200°C/400°F/gas mark 6.

Melt the butter with the olive oil in a roasting tin. Toss in the potatoes, lemon thyme and olives and season well. Roast until golden (25–30 minutes).

Meanwhile, pour the extra tbsp of olive oil into a hot nonstick frying pan. Lay the John Dory fillets, skin side down, in the oil and fry over a medium heat until the skin is well coloured and crisp (about 5 minutes). Turn the fillets over and roast for a further 8 minutes.

When the potatoes are cooked, toss the tarragon through using 2 wooden spoons.

To serve, arrange a mound of potatoes in the centre of each plate, place the fish on top and finish with a trail of salsa verde over the fish and a drizzle of extra virgin olive oil around the plate.

Steamed halibut with purple sprouting broccoli and black olives

Serves 4

1 tbsp extra virgin olive oil

4 halibut fillets, about
175g (6oz) each

200ml (7fl oz) fish stock

salt and pepper

Purple sprouting broccoli

750g (1lb 10oz) purple sprouting
broccoli

1 tbsp extra virgin olive oil

4 anchovy fillets

rind of 1 unwaxed lemon

200g (7oz) black olives, pitted

Black olive dressing

50g (1¾oz) black olives, pitted
and cut in half

100ml (3½fl oz) extra virgin
olive oil

Halibut steams very well: it holds its shape beautifully and happily takes on board all the flavours of the lemon, olives and stock. As it's quite a meaty fish, it can be served with purple sprouting broccoli, which is a fairly robust vegetable.

Bring a large saucepan of lightly salted water to the boil. When boiling, blanch the purple sprouting broccoli for about 5 minutes. Cool under cold running water and drain.

To dress the purple sprouting broccoli, heat the oil in a frying pan. Fry the anchovies and lemon rind until softened. Add the broccoli and black olives and fry over a medium–high heat. Stir to mix all the flavours together. When hot, turn out on to a plate. Set aside in a warm place.

To cook the halibut, heat the oil in a nonstick frying pan over a medium heat. Place the fish, skin side down, in the frying pan and apply gentle but firm pressure to the fillets to crisp the skin and gently cook the fish for about 5 minutes.

Turn the fillets over and pour in the fish stock. Bring to the boil and cover. Lower the heat and simmer for 5–8 minutes until the fish is flaky.

To make the black olive dressing, simply mix the olives and olive oil together.

Serve each fillet of halibut with some purple sprouting broccoli and black olive dressing.

Cod with rosemary-salted chips and tartare sauce

Serves 2

350g (12oz) Maris Piper potatoes, peeled and cut in half lengthways

2 cod fillets, about 200g (7oz) each, pin boned

1 tsp extra virgin olive oil

Tartare sauce

1 free-range egg, plus 1 free-range egg yolk

1 tsp Dijon mustard

1 tsp white wine vinegar

salt and pepper

100ml (3½ fl oz) extra virgin olive oil

1 garlic clove, crushed

1 tbsp chopped capers

1 tbsp chopped cornichons

3 anchovy fillets, chopped

1 small bunch of flat leaf parsley, finely chopped

juice of 1 lemon

Rosemary salt

3 sprigs of rosemary, leaves only

1 tbsp sea salt crystals

For me, breaking the rules is part of the buzz of cooking. Here's my Italian take on good old British fish 'n' chips: cod without any batter, roasted not fried; chunky chips cooked in olive oil and tossed in rosemary salt, all dished up with a tartare sauce spiked with anchovies, capers and cornichons. Hey! Why not?

Cut each half of potato into 3 chunky chips, cutting down at an angle to create triangular shapes. Put the chips into a large saucepan, cover with cold water and bring to the boil. Cook for 5 minutes, then drain through a colander. Spread the par-boiled chips out in a single layer on a baking sheet to cool.

If you have a deep-fat fryer, turn it on to high. If not, pour a good depth of vegetable oil into a large deep saucepan, leaving plenty of room to add the chips without the oil overflowing, and heat over a medium heat.

To make the tartare sauce, put the egg and egg yolk, mustard, vinegar, salt and pepper into a small mixing bowl and whisk for about 60 seconds until the mixture starts to thicken. Then drizzle in the olive oil very slowly, whisking all the time to form a thick mayonnaise. Stir in the rest of the ingredients until evenly distributed. Set aside.

To cook the cod, heat the olive oil in a nonstick frying pan over a medium heat. When the oil is hot, carefully place the cod, skin side down, in the pan and fry until the skin is crispy (about 5 minutes). Turn the fillets over and continue frying until cooked (4–5 minutes). Take off the heat and set aside.

Meanwhile, when the oil is hot, deep-fry the chips until golden and crisp.

To prepare the rosemary salt, put the rosemary and salt into a mortar and pound to a coarse paste with the pestle. Tip into a large bowl, add the chips and toss until evenly coated.

Serve the cod with a neat stack of triangular rosemary-salted chips and spoonfuls of the tartare sauce.

Lemon sole with anchovy and caper butter sauce

There's no need to overcomplicate this dish at all: wonderfully fresh fish simply baked in the oven with butter, anchovies, capers and lemon is perfection on a plate. To top it all, lemon sole is still one of the less expensive fine fish on the market and easy to get hold of all year round.

Serves 2

2 lemon sole, about 400g (14oz) each
salt and pepper
1 lemon, cut into 6 slices
dressed salad, to serve

Anchovy and caper butter sauce
6 anchovy fillets
2 tbsp capers
100g (3½oz) unsalted butter, softened
1 bunch of flat leaf parsley

Rinse the fish in cold water and pat dry with kitchen paper. Place one fish on a chopping board. With a sharp pair of kitchen scissors, trim away the frill around the edge of the fish. With a sharp knife, make a straight slit across the skin, a few millimetres from the tail fin on both sides of the fish. Starting on the dark-skin side, ease a finger under the slit to loosen a flap of skin large enough to grip firmly.

Use a clean tea towel to hold the fish tail down and to grip the flap of skin tightly. Slowly pull the skin towards the head. It should come away cleanly but, where it sticks, use fingers to release it to avoid tearing the fish. Do the same on the pale-skin side. Repeat for the second fish. Alternatively, leave the skin on and make 4 slashes in the flesh. Season the lemon soles with salt and pepper and set aside.

Preheat the oven to 180°C/350°F/gas mark 4.

Put all the ingredients for the anchovy and caper butter in a food processor and blitz until coarsely chopped.

Place the lemon soles on a large baking sheet and cover with the butter mixture. Lay 3 lemon slices along the back of each fish. Bake for 20–25 minutes.

Serve the lemon soles immediately with the melted butter sauce spooned over the top and a dressed salad on the side.

Monkfish with braised fennel, salami and salsa rossa piccante

Serves 2

100g (3½oz) salami Milano, thinly sliced

2 monkfish tails, about 150g (5½oz) each

salt and pepper

25g (1oz) butter

100ml (3½fl oz) fish stock or water

1 tbsp extra virgin olive oil

salsa *rossa piccante* (see page 121)

Braised fennel

1 tsp vegetable oil

2 bulbs of fennel, tough outer leaves removed, cut into quarters

1 star anise

125ml (4fl oz) white wine

1 chilli, deseeded and finely chopped

1 garlic clove, finely chopped

200g (7oz) leaf spinach, washed

1 x 400g can Italian chopped tomatoes

1 cinnamon stick

cracked black pepper

Believe it or not, in the 1970s fishermen used to throw monkfish back into the sea as a bad catch. Fortunately, since then, this lovely meaty fish has gained the respect it deserves and now appears on the very best of menus in luscious dishes like this.

To prepare the braised fennel, heat the vegetable oil in a large heavy-based braising pan or flameproof casserole over a medium heat and add the fennel and star anise. Fry until the fennel is browned all over (5–6 minutes), stirring occasionally to avoid burning.

Pour in the wine and cover with a lid. Reduce the heat and cook the fennel until tender (about 10 minutes). Add a little water if the pan looks as though it's boiling dry.

Turn the heat up and stir in the chilli, garlic and spinach. Cook for 2–3 minutes, turning the spinach over all the time with 2 wooden spoons, until the leaves wilt.

Pour in the tomatoes, toss in the cinnamon stick and season to taste with the pepper. Cook slowly, without a lid, over a low–medium heat for 15–20 minutes.

Meanwhile, fry the salami slices in a frying pan until the fat begins to melt. Transfer the salami to the braised fennel. Season the monkfish well and place in the frying pan. Raise the heat under the frying pan and drop in the butter. Turn the monkfish around in the melting butter to brown all over.

When golden brown, add the monkfish to the braised fennel and stir in the fish stock. Cover with a lid and simmer over a low heat for a further 10 minutes.

When the fish is cooked, remove the lid and taste to check the seasoning. Pick out the star anise and cinnamon stick and stir the extra virgin olive oil through the braised fennel.

Serve the monkfish on a bed of braised fennel and salami in salsa *rossa piccante*.

Seafood lasagne

Serves 4

200g (7oz) Basic egg pasta dough
(*see* page 25)

Sauce
150ml (¼ pint) single cream
200ml (7fl oz) fish stock
50g (1¾oz) unsalted butter
50g (1¾oz) plain flour

Seafood mixture
24 mussels, cleaned and debearded
24 clams, cleaned and debearded
2 tbsp olive oil
8 raw tiger prawns, shelled
and deveined
4 scallops
2 large tuna steaks, 2cm (¾in)
thick, cut into 2cm (¾in) cubes
1 red chilli, deseeded and finely
chopped
2 garlic cloves, finely chopped
1 large glass of white wine
handful of flat leaf parsley,
chopped
sprig of tarragon
salt and pepper

Pangrattato
1 ciabatta loaf, crusts removed, cut
into croûtons, toasted and blitzed
into breadcrumbs
25g (1oz) fennel seeds, lightly
toasted in a dry frying pan and
crushed
2 tsp dried chilli flakes

There are no rules for making this dish: the beauty is that it can be different every time you serve it. In this version, I've used a variety of fish and shellfish but there's nothing to stop you using a different selection of seafood. You can even vary the vegetables and herbs you use. It's entirely up to you.

To make the sauce, pour the cream and stock into a saucepan and bring to a simmer. Melt the butter in a saucepan and when it is foaming stir in the flour to form a paste. Take off the heat and very slowly begin to whisk in the hot cream and fish stock. As the sauce starts to thicken, return the saucepan to a low heat and slowly whisk in the remaining stock. Gently simmer the sauce over a low heat for 15 minutes to cook the flour. Set aside with a lid on the saucepan to stop a skin forming on top of the sauce.

Bring a large saucepan of lightly salted cold water to the boil.

Discard any mussels or clams that are open and fail to close when tapped against the side of the sink. Heat the olive oil in another large saucepan. Tip in the mussels and clams and fry briefly, giving the saucepan a good shake occasionally. Add the prawns and scallops and fry until the prawns start turning pink. Drop in the tuna and fry until lightly browned. Add the chilli and garlic and stir to let the flavours mingle. Pour in the wine and cook until completely evaporated before turning off the heat. Discard any mussels and clams that have not opened.

When the sauce is cooked, pour over the seafood and stir well. Mix in the herbs and taste to check the seasoning.

Roll out the pasta into 8 sheets on setting number 1 on the machine. Blanch the pasta sheets in the boiling water for 1–2 minutes, then drain.

Mix the *pangrattato* ingredients together in a large mixing bowl.

To serve, build up a stack of seafood and pasta. Place a spoonful of seafood mixture in the centre of 4 shallow bowls and lay a sheet of pasta over the top. Then spoon on more seafood mixture and top with a second sheet of pasta. Sprinkle over a little pangrattato for a crunchy finish.

Fish pie

Serves 4–6

2 cod, haddock or hake
fillets, about 500–600g
(1lb 2oz–1lb 5oz) each

1 undyed smoked haddock fillet,
about 250g (9oz)

1 celery stick, finely chopped

1 leek, cleaned and finely chopped

1 onion, finely chopped

2 bay leaves

200ml (7fl oz) double cream

400ml (14fl oz) fish stock

6 cooked tiger prawns, peeled

1 small bunch of chervil, leaves
only, finely chopped (optional)

70g (2½oz) unsalted butter

70g (2½oz) plain flour

Mashed potatoes

1kg (2lb 4oz) floury potatoes
(Maris Piper or King Edward),
peeled and roughly chopped

125g (4½oz) butter

salt and pepper

1 small bunch of flat leaf parsley,
leaves only, finely chopped

When you're making a fish pie, it's always a good idea to cut the fish into large chunks so that they stay whole and succulent. All you need to go with it are some well-seasoned steamed vegetables. I like to finish up any leftovers as a cold snack with a crunchy mixed leaf salad and beetroot.

Put the fish, vegetables and bay leaves in a saucepan and add the cream and fish stock. Bring to a simmer, cover, remove from the heat and set aside.

To prepare the mashed potatoes, put the potatoes in a saucepan, cover with cold water and add a pinch of salt. Bring to the boil over a high heat. Reduce the heat to low and simmer for about 15 minutes until tender.

When cooked, drain through a colander and return to the saucepan over a low heat. Stir with a wooden spoon to break up the potatoes while any remaining water evaporates. Mash the potatoes with the butter until smooth and season. Stir in the parsley and a little cooking liquid from the fish.

Preheat the oven to 200°C/400°F/gas mark 6.

Pass the fish liquid through a sieve into a bowl and set aside. Discard the vegetables and bay leaves. Carefully peel off the skin and flake the fish into a mixing bowl. Remove any bones. Add the prawns and, if you like, the chervil.

To make a sauce for the fish, melt the butter in a saucepan over a low heat and mix in the flour to form a paste. Start whisking in the fish cream, a little at a time. When all the liquid is incorporated, turn the heat right down and cook the sauce, stirring regularly, until thick, smooth and glossy (5–10 minutes).

To assemble the fish pie, pour the sauce over the flaked fish, stir, taste and season if necessary. Tip into a large baking dish.

Fill a large clean plastic sandwich bag with the mashed potato. Cut off the corner and pipe thick lines of potato over the fish mixture. Bake for 20 minutes until piping hot. Place under a hot grill until the top is golden and bubbling.

Sicilian fisherman's stew with lemon aïoli and tarragon

Serves 4

1 fillet of seabass, about 250g (9oz) with skin on, pin boned and cut into 4 pieces

350g (12oz) tuna steak, 2cm (¾in) thick, cut into 2cm (¾in) cubes

1 whole red mullet, about 300g (10½oz) with skin on, filleted and each fillet cut in half

salt and pepper

2 tbsp olive oil, plus extra for frying

20 clams or mussels, cleaned and debearded

8 raw tiger prawns, shelled and deveined

5 garlic cloves, 4 chopped, 1 halved

2 red chillies, deseeded and finely chopped

1 large wine glass Soave or another Italian dry white wine

400g (14oz) salsa *rossa piccante* (*see* page 121)

400ml (14fl oz) good-quality canned crab or lobster bisque or fresh fish stock

1 large pinch of saffron

200g (7oz) leaf spinach, washed

juice of 1 lemon

1 tbsp extra virgin olive oil

20g (¾oz) fennel tops (optional)

2 sprigs of tarragon, leaves only

Bruschetta

4 slices ciabatta

100g (3½oz) lemon aïoli (*see* page 154)

Tuscan olive oil for drizzling

Fish stews crop up a lot in Italian cooking because they're winning, must-try dishes, crammed full of such exciting flavours and colours. Usually when I make any kind of stew, I add some sort of dumpling as that's what I grew up with. For an Italian stew like this, gnocchi are perfect: they're light and soak up masses of those tasty juices.

Spread the prepared fish out on a chopping board and season. Drizzle with olive oil and work the seasoning and oil into the fish until evenly coated. Discard any clams or mussels that are open and fail to close when tapped against the side of the sink.

Heat a little olive oil in a large saucepan over a medium heat. Throw in the tiger prawns and fry until they start to turn pink. Add the fish pieces, the clams or mussels, chopped garlic and chilli. Reduce the heat slightly and carefully stir the seafood with a wooden spoon until it starts to colour (20–30 seconds).

Increase the heat again and deglaze the pan with the wine. Pour in the salsa *rossa* and the bisque or fish stock, saffron and spinach and bring to the boil. Cover the pan with a lid, reduce the heat to minimum and simmer for 10 minutes.

While the fish is cooking, preheat a griddle pan or grill to hot. Brush the slices of ciabatta with a little olive oil and toast on the preheated griddle or under the grill. Once grilled, rub the bruschetta with the cut side of the halved raw garlic clove and set aside.

When the seafood stew is cooked, discard any clams or mussels that have not opened. Taste, adjust the seasoning if necessary, and stir in the lemon juice.

Divide the seafood and spinach evenly between 4 bowls with a slotted spoon and ladle over plenty of sauce. (If the sauce is not thick enough, return the saucepan to the stove over maximum heat and boil vigorously to reduce and thicken a little.) Scatter over the fennel tops, if you like, and tarragon. Place a slice of bruschetta on each bowl and top with a spoonful of lemon aïoli. Finish with a drizzle of olive oil.

Mussels in salsa *rossa piccante*

In the UK, mussels are in their prime in November and December and it's well worth eating them when they're at their most plump and juicy. They take only a couple of minutes to cook: once the shells are open they're ready to eat.

Serves 4–6

2kg (4lb 8oz) fresh mussels, cleaned and debearded
bunch of tarragon
1 lemon, cut into wedges
crusty bread, to serve

Salsa *rossa piccante*
1 tbsp extra virgin olive oil
1 red chilli, deseeded and chopped
3 garlic cloves, sliced
2 x 400g cans Italian plum tomatoes
1 cinnamon stick
3 bay leaves
1 tsp dried oregano
salt and pepper
2 tbsp caster sugar
4 tbsp red wine vinegar

In a large saucepan big enough to hold all the mussels comfortably, start by making the salsa *rossa piccante*. Add the olive oil, chilli and garlic and fry over a medium heat for 1 minute.

Mix in the tomatoes, cinnamon, bay leaves, oregano and salt and pepper. Simmer for 15 minutes, stirring frequently.

Discard any mussels that are open and fail to close when tapped against the side of the sink.

Stir in the sugar and red wine vinegar. Bring the salsa *rossa piccante* back to the boil before tipping in the mussels. Cover with a lid and cook until the shells of the mussels have parted (about 5 minutes). Discard any mussels that have not opened. Discard the cinnamon stick and the bay leaves.

Tear in some fresh tarragon leaves and serve in bowls with plenty of crusty bread to mop up the juices and a wedge of lemon.

Lobster curry with fennel and polenta bread

Serves 4

2 live lobsters, about 550g
(1lb 4oz) each, killed by a
fishmonger or by the less
squeamish cooks (*see* page 34)

900g (2lb) canned Italian chopped
tomatoes

2 tbsp coconut oil or groundnut oil

2 onions, finely sliced

3 garlic cloves, finely sliced

3 green chillies, deseeded and
finely chopped

3 red chillies, deseeded and
finely chopped

10 curry leaves

1 tbsp turmeric

50g (1¾oz) tomato purée

1 x 250g can coconut milk

1 lemon, cut in half

4 tbsp unsalted cashew nuts

8 Anya potatoes, cut in half
and parboiled

1 small bunch of flat leaf parsley,
finely chopped

Fennel and polenta bread
(see page 180), to serve

Garam masala

1 tsp each ground cinnamon,
ground cloves, ground nutmeg,
ground cumin, ground coriander,
turmeric, garlic powder, sesame
seeds, black mustard seeds,
fennel seeds

2 bay leaves

1 green cardamom pod

1 tsp ground ginger

'How do curries relate to Italian cuisine?' I hear you ask. Well, hundreds of years ago many spices were introduced to Italy from Morocco and the Far East by Venetian traders and used as currency to buy salt, which was worth more than gold at the time. Exotic spices have been part of the cooking scene in Italy ever since.

To prepare the garam masala, toast all the spices and herbs, apart from the cardamom and ginger, in a dry heavy-based frying pan. When lightly toasted and releasing a spicy aroma, transfer to a pestle and mortar and pound together with the ginger and the black seeds in the cardamom pod, discarding the pod itself.

Place a large empty saucepan over a high heat until scorching hot (5–10 minutes). Carefully tip in the chopped tomatoes. When the popping subsides, stir briskly to avoid burning, then turn down the heat and simmer gently.

Heat the coconut oil in a large saucepan and sweat the onions, garlic, chillies, curry leaves and turmeric over a low heat until the onions are softened but not browned (about 15 minutes). Add the tomato purée and fry for 2–3 minutes, stirring all the time.

Split each lobster in half lengthways and crack the shells on the claws with a sharp tap from the back of a heavy knife or cleaver. Fry the lobster halves with the onion until the shells start to turn pink (about 5 minutes).

Add the reduced chopped tomatoes, coconut milk, lemon halves, cashew nuts and parboiled potatoes. Cook the lobster for 9–10 minutes then remove from the saucepan and simmer the sauce to thicken if necessary.

Discard any large pieces in the garam masala and stir the powder into the sauce.

Serve half a lobster per person in a bowl with sauce spooned over and garnished with parsley. Serve with Fennel and Polenta Bread to mop up the spicy juices.

Female lobsters are generally heavier and better value for money than male lobsters of the same size. Many experts claim that they also have a better flavour than the male. However, you may need an expert to tell you the difference between them!

Pan-seared scallops with celeriac mash, Swiss chard and pancetta

Serves 4

8 diver-caught scallops, shelled,
with beards and roes removed

salt and pepper

8 slices pancetta

1 tbsp olive oil

25g (1oz) butter

Celeriac mash

2 large King Edward potatoes,
peeled and cut into 2.5cm (1in)
cubes

25g (1oz) butter

1 whole celeriac, peeled and cut
into 2.5cm (1in) cubes

100ml (3½ fl oz) whole milk

100ml (3½ fl oz) double cream

splash of white truffle oil
(optional)

Swiss chard

4 large Swiss chard leaves, stalks
removed and cut into batons,
washed and drained in a colander

1 tbsp olive oil

2 garlic cloves, finely chopped

1 red chilli, deseeded and finely
chopped

It's always best to buy diver-caught King scallops if you can get hold of them. They're wonderfully plump and juicy and have been handled with care.

For the celeriac mash, heat a small saucepan of lightly salted cold water. Boil the potatoes until soft.

Meanwhile, melt the butter in a heavy-based saucepan over a medium heat and fry the celeriac until golden. Reduce the heat and add the milk and cream. Cover and cook until soft. Top up with water to stop the saucepan from boiling dry.

While the potatoes and celeriac are cooking, season the scallops and cut each into 2 large discs, giving 16 pieces in total. Put another larger saucepan of lightly salted cold water on to boil.

Drain the potatoes and return to the saucepan over a low heat. Break up with a wooden spoon while any remaining water evaporates. Drain the celeriac, saving the stock, and mash with the potatoes, seasoning well. Add enough stock to make the mash smooth and glossy. Cover and set aside.

Blanch the chard leaves and stalks in the saucepan of boiling water until tender (3–4 minutes). Drain. Heat the olive oil in a frying pan and fry the garlic and chilli over a low–medium heat until softened (3–4 minutes). Add the chard and toss well. Season well and set aside.

Lay the pancetta on a baking sheet and place under a medium grill to crisp up without burning (7–8 minutes).

Heat a heavy-based frying pan until very hot. Coat the half-scallops in the olive oil and fry for 1 minute until browned. Turn each half-scallop over, add the butter to the frying pan and fry for another minute before removing from the heat.

Before serving, reheat the mash, mixing in more stock if necessary to make it smooth and creamy. To serve, place a spoonful of celeriac mash and some chard on 4 large plates. Arrange 4 half-scallops and 2 slices of crisp pancetta on top.

Salt cod al forno

Serves 4

1 side of salt cod, soaked for
2 days in cold water that is
changed twice a day

450g (1lb) Charlotte potatoes,
sliced

cracked black pepper

6 tbsp olive oil

20g (¾oz) unsalted butter,
softened

2 garlic cloves, finely sliced

100g (3½oz) pitted black olives

handful of parsley leaves,
finely chopped

2 sprigs of thyme, leaves only

100g (3½oz) fresh white
breadcrumbs

I first had this dish in a wonderful little deli in London when I was just starting to get into food. I popped in out of curiosity and they let me taste their salt cod *al forno* from the antipasti trolley. I was blown away. I was even lucky enough to be given the recipe.

Preheat the oven to 180°C/350°F/gas mark 4.

After the cod has been soaking for 2 days, drain off the water and remove the skin and bones. Flake the cod into a bowl and set it aside in the refrigerator.

Heat a large saucepan of lightly salted cold water. Boil the potatoes until just tender (about 5–7 minutes), drain and season with pepper. Toss in 1 tbsp of the olive oil to stop the slices from sticking together.

Butter a medium-sized, deep baking sheet and spread a layer of potato over the bottom. Scatter some of the garlic, black olives, parsley, thyme, pepper and salt cod over the top. Arrange another layer of potatoes on top and repeat until all the ingredients are used up, finishing with a layer of potatoes.

Poke a finger down through the layers at 4cm (1½in) intervals all over the top, pour over the remaining olive oil and sprinkle on the breadcrumbs. Bake for 1 hour until golden. Serve the salt cod *al forno* as a starter or as an accompaniment to another fish dish.

barbecues
& snacks

The unpredictable British weather doesn't stop us from enjoying a good old barbecue now and then. The last barbecue I had was in my partner Nicci's mum's garden, which is just a stone's throw away from the Queen's Park Rangers' stadium in White City, west London. The team were playing a match that afternoon and we could have made some money on the side selling barbecued hot dogs to the supporters, they were that close.

It was raining, as it usually does in the UK in April, but that didn't dampen our enthusiasm. The barbeque was in full flow – all we were missing was a family-sized umbrella! Come rain, sleet or snow, there's always time for a barbecue. And what better occasion to try out some of the recipes in this chapter?

Boned leg of spring lamb, rubbed with rosemary and garlic marinade with flatbreads and Moroccan couscous

Serves 8

1 leg of lamb, about
3kg (6lb 8oz), boned and
butterflied by a butcher
1 batch of flatbreads
(*see* Flatbread pizzas, page 146)

Rosemary and garlic marinade

5 sprigs of fresh rosemary
1 garlic bulb, cut in half around
the middle
juice and rind of 1 unwaxed lemon
sea salt crystals and cracked
black pepper
50ml (2fl oz) olive oil

Moroccan couscous

100g (3½oz) raisins, soaked
overnight in 100ml (3½fl oz)
Vin Santo
500g (1lb 2oz) couscous
1 tbsp extra virgin olive oil
seeds from ½ pomegranate
1 bunch of flat leaf parsley,
chopped
500ml (18fl oz) meat stock
100g (3½oz) unsalted butter
at room temperature
sea salt crystals and cracked
black pepper

This is a real crowd-pleaser. Practically all you have to do is throw a whole leg of lamb on the barbecue to produce a feast to delight all your friends and family. Another nice way to serve it is to spread crème fraîche on the flatbread, top with slices of lamb and couscous and roll it up like a wrap. But take a tip from one who knows: get the barbecue going early as the lamb takes a while to cook.

Rub the lamb all over with the rosemary, garlic, lemon rind and salt and pepper. Then rub in the olive oil and half the lemon juice. Leave to marinate for at least 2–3 hours or overnight in the refrigerator, turning occasionally.

After marinating, remove the lamb from the marinade, pat dry with kitchen paper and season well. Set aside to come to room temperature. Meanwhile, heat the barbecue or griddle until hot.

To prepare the Moroccan couscous, mix all the ingredients, apart from the stock, butter and salt and pepper, in a large bowl. Pour the stock into a saucepan and bring to a simmer.

Grill or barbecue the leg of lamb for 12–15 minutes on each side. (Allow 12 minutes for meat that is pink in the centre, 15 minutes if you prefer it well done.) Remove from the heat and transfer to a large platter or carving board. Squeeze over the remaining lemon juice and cover with kitchen foil. Let the lamb rest for 15 minutes or more in a warm place.

Put the uncooked flatbreads on the barbecue and cook for a minute on each side to brand with bar marks.

Pour the hot stock into the couscous and stir in the butter and some pepper. Mix thoroughly and cover tightly with clingfilm. After 2–3 minutes, remove the clingfilm, fluff up the couscous with a fork and adjust the seasoning to taste.

Slice and serve with the flatbreads and Moroccan couscous.

Italian beefburgers with tomato relish

Serves 8

1.3kg (3lb) lean steak mince

2 garlic cloves, pressed

1 bunch of parsley, finely chopped

2 sprigs of rosemary, leaves only, chopped

2 free-range egg yolks

100g (3½oz) Parmesan cheese, grated

½ nutmeg, grated

large pinch of dried chilli flakes

salt and pepper

Mini focaccias, to serve

Tomato relish

2 tbsp extra virgin olive oil

2 red onions, finely sliced

2 garlic cloves, finely chopped

1 apple, peeled, cored and chopped

25g (1oz) sugar

250g (9oz) cherry tomatoes, dunked in boiling water for 2 seconds and skinned

300g (10½oz) canned Italian chopped tomatoes

1 small bunch of mint, leaves only, chopped

Although I'm a chef now, I'm still just like the next person when it comes to fast food. I've been known to have the occasional fast food burger but I promise they'll never taste the same again after you've made your own burgers. And brewing up your own tomato relish beats ketchup any day.

To prepare the tomato relish, heat the olive oil in a saucepan and fry the onions and garlic over a low heat for 15 minutes. Add the apple, sugar, cherry tomatoes and canned tomatoes. Simmer gently until sweet and jam-like (about 40 minutes). Stir in the mint and season to taste.

To make the beefburgers, mix all the ingredients together thoroughly in a mixing bowl. Shape into 175g (6oz) balls, then flatten into burgers. Alternatively, press the beef mixture into one thick slab and stamp out 16 neat burgers with a 7.5cm (3in) ring (an empty tuna can with the top and bottom removed is ideal).

Cook the burgers on the barbecue for 5 minutes on each side, or a little longer for better done. Serve with the delicious sweet tomato relish and Mini focaccias (*see* page 194).

Barbecued belly pork with salsa verde

Serves 8

1 whole pork belly, off the bone

50g (1¾oz) fennel seeds, lightly toasted in a dry frying pan

20g (¾oz) dried chilli flakes

1 tbsp sea salt crystals

1 tbsp cracked black pepper

3 tbsp olive oil

3 tbsp red wine vinegar

Salsa verde

1 bunch of parsley, leaves only, finely chopped

1 bunch of mint, leaves only, finely chopped

1 bunch of oregano, leaves only, finely chopped

1 handful of capers, finely chopped

1 handful of baby gherkins, finely chopped

1 tsp Dijon mustard

1 large garlic clove, finely chopped

2 tbsp red wine vinegar

50ml (2fl oz) olive oil

salt and pepper

Belly of pork is the cheapest cut of pork but definitely has the best flavour. This is due to its high fat content, which adds flavour to the meat. Salsa verde is a sauce full of character and acidic flavours that help cut through the fat. For the best result, cut the pork belly in half lengthways and, when barbecuing, place a roasting tray over the top to form a makeshift oven that will ensure the pork is cooked through.

Preheat the oven to 180°C/350°F/gas mark 4. Any roasting should be started 3 hours before the barbecue.

Slash the skin of the belly at 2cm (¾in) intervals with a sharp knife, first horizontally then vertically.

Grind the fennel seeds and chilli flakes together with the sea salt and cracked pepper. Rub all over the pork belly, working the spices well into the cuts in the skin.

Grease a baking sheet large enough to hold the whole pork belly with the olive oil and warm over a high heat.

Put the pork onto the sheet, skin side down. Turn the heat down low and fry for 15 minutes. When the skin is golden and starting to crisp up, brush on the red wine vinegar and place the pork in the oven to roast for 2½ hours.

Meanwhile, mix all the ingredients for the salsa verde together in a mixing bowl. Set aside in the refrigerator.

When the belly is cooked through and tender, remove it from the oven and set aside to rest and cool slightly. When cool enough to handle, cut the pork into 2cm (¾in) thick strips. Set aside in the refrigerator until needed.

When the time comes, place the pork strips on a hot barbecue and grill for 3 minutes on each side. Serve immediately with the salsa verde.

Fillets of seabass stuffed with summer herbs

Serves 6

12 fillets of seabass, pin boned
by a fishmonger
salt and pepper
1 bunch of purple basil
1 bunch of green basil
1 bunch of sorrel
1 bunch of oregano
1 bunch of wild fennel tops
3 tbsp extra virgin olive oil
juice of 1 lemon

To serve
aïoli (*see* page 154)
mixed salad leaves

These tasty stuffed seabass fillets are great for summer barbecues, and dead easy to prepare. If you are planning a picnic barbecue away from home, prepare the parcels in advance, adding a knob of butter to each one and seasoning generously with salt and pepper. The parcels allow the fish to retain all their juices, and once cooked you can eat them straight out of the foil.

Lay 6 fillets of seabass skin side down on a chopping board. Season well and arrange a sprig of each herb on every fillet. Place a second fillet on top of the herbs, skin side up and tie the fillets together with butcher's twine. Alternatively, skewer the fillets together to keep the herbs away from the heat.

Brush both skin sides of the parcels lightly with the olive oil and place on the barbecue. Cook for 5–6 minutes on each side.

Heat the rest of the olive oil gently in a foil tray over a cool part of the barbecue.

When the fish is beginning to char on the outside, transfer it to the warm olive oil and squeeze over the lemon juice. Rest at this lower temperature for a few minutes, turning occasionally, so that the centres of the parcels can finish cooking without burning the skin any more.

Serve with a little aïoli and some mixed salad leaves.

Whole seabream stuffed with lemon, rosemary and basil

Serves 8

8 seabream, about 300g (10½oz)
each, or 4 seabream, about 600g
(1lb 5oz) each, scaled and gutted
salt and pepper
2 tsp olive oil
4 unwaxed lemons, each cut
into 4 wedges
8 garlic cloves, smashed
8 sprigs of rosemary
1 large of bunch basil, leaves only

To serve
extra virgin olive oil for drizzling
fennel tops (optional)

This fish dish has a lot going for it: really easy to make, full of flavour and ideal for barbecuing. You can really taste the rosemary coming through. It's a good tip to score the fish first as it can help you to see when it's cooked.

Light the barbecue well in advance, so that when the time comes to cook the fish there are no flames, just white hot coals.

With a sharp knife, make 3 deep cuts into the thickest part of the fish on both sides. Season all the cuts and inside the cavity. Rub a little olive oil over the fish.

Place a lemon wedge, 1 or 2 garlic cloves, a sprig of rosemary and a handful of basil leaves into the cavity of each fish. Twisting the rosemary first helps to release its aromatic oils. If necessary, tie a piece of butcher's twine around the middle of the fish to keep the flavourings inside.

Place the prepared fish on the barbecue and cook for 4–5 minutes on each side, depending on the size of the fish. To check if the fish is cooked, pull the flesh at the thickest part near the head: it should be opaque all the way through and come away from the bone easily.

Gently transfer the cooked fish to a serving platter. Squeeze the remaining lemon wedges over the fish and drizzle over some extra virgin olive oil. Garnish with feathery fennel tops if you like.

Red mullet with grilled spring garlic

Fresh spring garlic has a sensational flavour, much mellower than the drier cloves that are normally used for cooking. I like to grill spring garlic, dress it with lemon and extra virgin olive oil and serve it with lamb or fish. The combination of mild and subtle flavours is a marriage made in heaven.

Serves 6

4 bulbs of fresh spring or 'wet' garlic, cut into quarters
500ml (15fl oz) rape seed or vegetable oil
6 red mullet, about 300g (10½oz) each, scaled and gutted by a fishmonger
salt and pepper
6 sprigs of thyme
3 tbsp extra virgin olive oil
juice of 1 lemon

Place the quartered garlic in a saucepan with the oil and heat very gently over a pilot light or a very low heat for 3–4 hours to soften the garlic and mellow any harsh raw flavours.

Make 3 slashes in the sides of each fish and season on the outside and inside the cavity. Place a sprig of thyme inside each fish and set aside.

Drain the spring garlic. Brush a little of the oil over the fish and save the rest for future cooking.

Always wait for the flames on the barbecue to die down before cooking. Place the fish on the barbecue and cook for 15–20 minutes, turning once.

After turning the fish, put the spring garlic on the barbecue.

Remove the cooked fish from the barbecue with a spatula and transfer to a warm serving dish. Serve immediately with the spring garlic, a drizzle of extra virgin olive oil and the lemon juice.

Seafood spiedini with onions and peppers

No barbecue is complete without kebabs and I like to jazz them up with some of my favourite seafood. My girlfriend's mum, Dee, loves these *spiedinis* made with onions and mixed peppers but it's up to you which vegetables or fruit you use: tomatoes, courgettes, fennel or lemons are all good with seafood.

Serves 4

8 large raw prawns, shelled and deveined
2 red peppers, cored, deseeded and cut into chunks
8 large scallops
1 red onion, cut into chunks and broken up into layers
2 swordfish or tuna steaks, at least 4cm (1½ in) thick, cut into 4cm (1½ in) cubes
salt and pepper
3 tbsp extra virgin olive oil

Butter sauce

3 tbsp unsalted butter
125ml (4fl oz) white wine
200ml (7fl oz) chicken stock
1 bunch of parsley, finely chopped

Soak some wooden skewers in water overnight before using for the *spiedini* to prevent them from burning.

To prepare the *spiedini*, thread 1 prawn, a piece of red pepper, 1 scallop, a piece of onion, 1 cube of fish and a piece of red pepper on to each of 4 skewers. Continue loading the skewers until there are 2 pieces of every item of seafood on each. Season well, rub all over with the olive oil and set aside.

Place a small saucepan on the barbecue, add the butter in small pieces and melt until foaming. Pour in the wine and reduce until completely evaporated before adding the chicken stock. Leave to simmer gently.

While the sauce is simmering, grill the *spiedini* until cooked (about 3 minutes on each side). Remove from the barbecue.

Whisk the parsley into the butter sauce and spoon a little over the spiedini. Serve immediately.

Barbecued squid with chilli jam dip

I love barbecued squid. I think grilling it over charcoal is the best way to cook it. You get a lovely smoky flavour and nice crunchy bits. Sweet chilli jam dip is another must at my barbecues: it delivers such a smooth spicy blast. Fortunately, it keeps for up to a month in the fridge, so there's plenty of time to enjoy the lot.

Serves 6

18 small squid, cleaned and prepared

1 tbsp extra virgin olive oil

2 garlic cloves, chopped

1 red chilli, finely chopped

juice of 1 lemon

salt and pepper

Chilli jam dip

2 or 3 pasilla chillies (also known as negro chillies) or 2 or 3 fresh red chillies

2 or 3 green chillies

10 garlic cloves

6cm (2½in) fresh root ginger, peeled

250ml (9fl oz) red wine vinegar

1 x 200g can Italian chopped tomatoes

50ml (2fl oz) Thai fish sauce (*nam pla*)

250g (9oz) caster sugar

To make the chilli jam dip, blend the chillies, garlic, ginger and red wine vinegar to a paste in a food processor.

Tip into a saucepan and stir in the tomatoes and fish sauce. Bring to the boil and skim off any scum from the top before stirring in the caster sugar. Simmer over a low heat until the jam thickens.

When the jam is ready, grill the squid on a hot barbecue or griddle for 3 minutes, turning over once, until there are clear bar marks on both sides.

Heat the extra virgin olive oil in a frying pan and toss in the squid, garlic and chilli. Mix well, then add a generous squeeze of lemon juice to the frying pan.

Leave the squid to rest for 2–3 minutes before serving with the chilli jam dip.

Flatbread pizzas

Makes about 10 pizzas

Tomato sauce

1kg (2lb 4oz) cherry tomatoes

3 garlic cloves, crushed

100ml (3½ fl oz) extra virgin olive oil

1 bunch of basil, leaves only

salt and pepper

Flatbreads

600ml (1 pint) tepid water

2 x 7g sachets fast-action dried yeast

1 tbsp caster sugar

1 tbsp extra virgin olive oil

1kg (2lb 4oz) tipo '00' flour or pizza flour, plus extra for dusting

1 tbsp salt

salt and pepper

I remember making these in Cumbria on a sourcing trip with Fifteen. We were sitting around a fire, cooking a variety of treats and wishing we had some bread to go with them. Quick as a flash, I came up with this dough, which we flattened out and cooked quickly over the flames. Then we whacked whatever we had on top like a pizza and everyone was satisfied.

To make the tomato sauce, tip the tomatoes, garlic and olive oil into a saucepan and cook over a medium heat until the tomatoes have collapsed to a pulp (about 30 minutes). Tear in the basil leaves and season to taste. Cover with a lid and set aside in a warm place. Store any leftover sauce in a refrigerator.

To make the pizza bases, mix the warm water, yeast, sugar and olive oil together in a jug. Then sift the flour and salt together into a large bowl. Make a well in the centre and pour in the water mixture. Mix and knead the mixture together to form a pliable dough.

Divide the dough into 10 pieces, each about the size of a tennis ball. Cover with a damp cloth and leave in a warm place for about 20 minutes to rise.

When well risen, dust a clean work surface or chopping board with a little flour and roll the balls out into flat discs with a rolling pin.

Throw the dough discs on to the barbecue or griddle and lightly toast on both sides. Remove from the heat and spread a little warm tomato sauce on top.

Scatter over your favourite toppings while the flatbread is still hot. Some of mine include mozzarella and prosciutto; barbecued mushrooms and Pecorino; black olives and Parmesan shavings; salami Milano and rocket; smoked salmon and horseradish; and ricotta and crisp pancetta.

salads &
antipasti

There are so many unusual salad ingredients available nowadays that the traditional British trio of tomatoes, lettuce and cucumber seems a little bland in comparison. So why not spruce up your salads by sampling some of the other delicious ingredients that are on offer?

To start with, there is a plethora of alternate salad leaves – bitter leaves such as dandelion, radicchio di Treviso, beet leaves (I particularly love Bull's Blood baby beet leaves with their distinctive red colouration), chicory, radicchio and countless more. These bitter leaves all work well with fruit as they balance the sweet flavours.

Traditional Italian antipasti consists of a selection of cured meats, cheeses and marinated vegetables – this is still a popular starter in many Italian trattorias.

Mozzarella salad with prosciutto di Parma, melon and pistachios

The idea of combining meat, fruit and cheese on one plate may sound a bit strange but the Italians pull off this beautiful marriage of flavours and textures brilliantly. It's particularly worth serving when melons are bang in season and at their juiciest: catch all those lovely juices to make a smashing dressing.

Serves 4

4 balls of buffalo mozzarella, about 125g (4½oz) each
vinaigrette (*see* page 171)
salt and pepper
1 small ripe charentais or cantaloupe melon, halved and deseeded with a spoon
8 slices of prosciutto *di Parma* or prosciutto *di San Daniele*
100g (3½oz) salted pistachio nuts, shelled and lightly crushed
50g (1¾oz) rocket leaves

To serve
small handful of basil leaves
Tuscan extra virgin olive oil for drizzling
aged balsamic vinegar for drizzling
Parmesan cheese shavings (optional)

Remove the mozzarella from the refrigerator 30 minutes before serving. Let it come to room temperature and drain off the liquid. Tear each ball into 3 or 4 large pieces and arrange on 4 plates. Drizzle over a little vinaigrette and season lightly with salt and pepper.

To scoop out crescent-shaped pieces of melon, dig the side of a dessertspoon deep into the flesh and lift out a neatly curved spoonful. Season the melon with black pepper and carefully arrange on top of the mozzarella.

Drape 2 slices of prosciutto over and around the melon on each plate. Scatter the pistachio nuts over the salad.

Toss the rocket with a little vinaigrette. Divide between the plates.

Tear and scatter the basil leaves around the plates. Drizzle over the olive oil and balsamic vinegar. Finish with a few shavings of Parmesan, if you like.

Sliced pork with tuna sauce

Serves 4–8

1 Rolled loin of pork stuffed
with dried apricots and sage
(*see* page 68)

Tuna sauce

300g (10½oz) belly of fresh tuna
½ bulb of garlic
3 bay leaves
1 sprig of rosemary
1 red chilli, pricked
½ cinnamon stick, crushed
250ml (8fl oz) vegetable oil
juice of ½ lemon
splash of white wine vinegar
salt and pepper

Aïoli

1 free-range egg
salt and ground white pepper
1 tsp Dijon mustard
½ garlic clove, finely grated
100ml (3½fl oz) vegetable oil
100ml (3½fl oz) olive oil

To serve

1 large red chilli, deseeded and
finely chopped
100g (3½oz) rocket

L'arista di maiale con salsa tonnata, to give this dish its full Italian title, is probably my favourite starter. When I go out to eat, I order it wherever and whenever I see it on the menu. It's just an uncanny combination that throws me. Who'd have thought that pork and tuna would go so well together? Seriously, when you try it, you'll understand what I mean.

Put the tuna, garlic, herbs and spices in a small saucepan and pour in enough vegetable oil to cover the fish. Cook the tuna very slowly and gently over a pilot light for about an hour or until the fish is opaque and flaky. (In the absence of a pilot light, put the saucepan over a low heat until the oil is warm to the touch then switch off the heat. Periodically apply short bursts of gentle heat until the tuna is cooked.) Remove the cooked tuna from the oil and drain on kitchen paper to remove any excess oil.

To make the aïoli, put the egg, a pinch of salt, a pinch of white pepper, the mustard and garlic in a large mixing bowl. If you have someone helping you, ask them to hold the bowl as you work, as you will need both hands. Alternatively, wedge the bowl securely in the top of a saucepan with a tea towel. Whisk until the egg has increased in volume. Slowly add the vegetable oil in a thin steady stream, whisking continuously, until the mixture has thickened. Use one hand to whisk, one to pour the oil. Slowly add the olive oil in a thin stream, whisking all the time, to form a thick garlicky mayonnaise. For lemon aïoli, add the juice of 1 lemon after the olive oil.

Tip the drained tuna into a food processor and blend to a paste. Stir into the aïoli. Check the flavour and add lemon juice, white wine vinegar and salt and pepper to taste. Set aside in the refrigerator.

Using a very sharp carving knife, slice the loin of pork as thinly as possible.

Distribute the sliced pork evenly between the plates and serve with 2 spoonfuls of tuna mayonnaise. Garnish each plate with a few pieces of chilli and some rocket leaves.

Salami misti

A mouthwatering selection of cured meats with olives, capers, gherkins and Parmesan really is a blast of Italy on a plate.

Serves 4

8 thin slices of prosciutto *di Parma*

8 thin slices of *bresaola Punta d'anca* (air-dried beef from northern Italy)

8 thin slices of salami Milano

8 thin slices of *Copa de Parma* (salami)

12 large Cerignola olives from Puglia

100g (3½oz) Parmesan cheese, shaved

handful of capers

handful of cornichons (miniature French gherkins)

highest-quality extra virgin olive oil

fresh crusty bread, to serve

Simply bring everything up to room temperature, arrange attractively on a platter or individual plates and serve with a liberal glug of extra virgin olive oil and plenty of fresh crusty bread.

Grilled pigeon breast with coleslaw

Serves 4

8 pigeon breasts, off the bone
salt and pepper
1 tbsp extra virgin olive oil
2 garlic cloves, sliced
2 sprigs of thyme
20g (¾oz) unsalted butter
50ml (2fl oz) meat stock

Coleslaw

1 small white cabbage, quartered,
core removed and finely sliced,
then soaked in cold water for
30 minutes
2 carrots, peeled and coarsely
grated
1 small onion, very finely sliced
2 red apples, peeled, cored and
finely sliced
juice of ½ lemon
300ml (½ pint) mayonnaise
salt and pepper

This dish makes a fantastic and novel starter. Pigeon is enjoyed in the more rural areas of Italy, where the locals head out to shoot the birds in and around the month of November. It's best to cook pigeon medium to medium–rare, to ensure that it is juicy and full of flavour.

To make the coleslaw, drain the cabbage and tip into a large mixing bowl. Add the carrot, onion and apple, mix thoroughly and toss with the lemon juice. Stir in the mayonnaise until everything is well coated. Season to taste with salt and pepper.

To cook the pigeon breasts, heat a griddle pan until scorching hot and preheat the oven to 220°C/425°F/gas mark 7.

Place the pigeon breasts on a chopping board. Season well and rub in the oil. Lay each breast on the griddle and grill until well bar-marked (about 30 seconds on each side) to give a lightly charred flavour.

Spread the garlic, thyme and butter in the bottom of flameproof baking dish and lay the pigeon breasts on top without touching each other. Roast in the oven for 3 minutes, then rest the pigeon breasts on kitchen paper.

Meanwhile, deglaze the baking dish with the meat stock over a high heat. Pass through a sieve into another dish and return the breasts to the stock.

To serve, place the pigeon breasts on 4 plates, drizzle a little sauce over the top and add a spoonful of coleslaw.

Grilled sardines with agra dolce dressing

Serves 4 as a starter

4 sardines, about 175g (6oz) each,
or 8 if smaller, cleaned and gutted,
with gills removed

100ml (3½ fl oz) Tuscan extra
virgin olive oil

salt and pepper

1 unwaxed lemon, cut into
8 wedges

4 woody sprigs of rosemary

4 slices of good bread,
about 1cm (½ in) thick

1 garlic clove, cut in half

chicory leaves

Agra dolce (sweet-and-sour) dressing

60g (2¼ oz) raisins, soaked
in 2 tbsp red wine vinegar
for about 1 hour

100g (3½ oz) pine nuts, lightly
toasted in a dry frying pan

1 small handful of flat leaf parsley
leaves, roughly chopped

1 small handful of mint leaves,
roughly chopped

1 small handful of rocket leaves

8 large caper berries, cut in half

Fresh sardines come in different sizes so you can enjoy this dish either as a starter or a main course. In my eyes, the best way to cook these little fish is over an open fire in the same way as the street cooks do in the south of Italy. Served with a simple sweet–and–sour dressing like this they're well tasty.

Warm a heavy griddle pan over a high heat.

Rub a little of the olive oil over the sardines and season inside and out. Place a lemon wedge inside each sardine, skewering it in place with a sprig of rosemary.

Brush the remaining olive oil over each slice of bread and rub in well. When the griddle pan is scorching hot, toast the bread on both sides until branded with clear bar marks. Rub the cut face of the garlic over the toasted slices and set aside on a wire rack to stop the bruschetta sweating and becoming soft. Keep in a warm place.

Brush the crumbs off the griddle and return to the heat. When scorching hot again, turn the heat down and grill the sardines for about 3 minutes on each side.

While the sardines are grilling, mix all ingredients for the *agra dolce* dressing together in a small bowl.

As soon as the sardines are cooked, place the bruschetta on a plate and top with a couple of chicory leaves. Place the sardines on top of the chicory, spoon over the *agra dolce* dressing and serve immediately.

Fried whitebait with lemon, parsley and paprika mayo

Serves 6–8 as a starter

100g (3½ oz) plain flour

50g (1¾ oz) paprika

400g (14oz) whitebait

1 litre (1¾ pints) vegetable oil for frying

pinch of sea salt crystals

1 handful of flat leaf parsley leaves, roughly chopped

2 lemons, cut into quarters

Paprika mayo

1 large free-range egg

1 tsp Dijon mustard

100ml (3½ fl oz) vegetable oil

100ml (3½ fl oz) olive oil

1 tbsp white wine vinegar

1 tsp paprika

salt and pepper

squeeze of lemon juice (optional)

Back in the 19th century, fried whitebait was one of the earliest and most popular lunches to be had in inns all down the east coast of England. Although these baby herring are delicious on their own, I like to throw things up in the air a bit and serve them with a spicy paprika mayo or add an Italian tingle with some lemon aïoli.

To make the paprika mayo, whisk the egg and mustard together in a large bowl. Slowly drizzle in the oils, whisking continuously, until all the oil has been incorporated and the mixture has thickened. (It helps to have an extra pair of hands at this stage, with one person pouring while the other is whisking.) Stir in the vinegar and paprika. Season to taste and mix in a little lemon juice, if you like.

Sift the flour and paprika together into a large bowl. Tip in the whitebait and toss about until all the little fish are lightly dusted with spicy flour.

Pour the oil into a large deep saucepan and heat to frying temperature (190°C/375°F). Line another large bowl with kitchen paper to absorb any excess oil from the fish after frying.

When the oil is hot enough, fry small batches of the whitebait until crisp (about 5 minutes each time). Let the oil come back up to frying temperature between batches.

Remove from the oil with a slotted spoon and transfer to the paper-lined bowl. Sprinkle with sea salt and parsley.

Serve on individual plates with a wedge of lemon and a bowl of paprika mayo.

Tuna confit with soft-boiled egg and pancetta dressing

Serves 4

4 large free-range eggs
mixed salad leaves, to garnish

Tuna confit

400g (14oz) tuna belly
1 red chilli, pricked
2 garlic cloves, smashed in their skins
1 sprig of rosemary, twisted to release the flavours
1 sprig of thyme, twisted to release the flavours
1 star anise, smashed
vegetable oil to cover all the ingredients

Pancetta dressing

6 slices pancetta or streaky bacon, about 5mm (½in) thick, cut into lardons
2 tbsp aged balsamic vinegar
juice of ½ lemon
3 tbsp extra virgin olive oil

A lot like a traditional French Salade Niçoise, this dish has an unusual combination of flavours: the taste and texture of the tuna complements the smoky pancetta and the runny egg yolk beautifully. The great bonus of cooking the tuna in this way is that it keeps well in the fridge and you can make fabulous tuna mayo with it.

To prepare the confit, place the tuna, chill, garlic, herbs and star anise in a saucepan large enough to hold them comfortably. Cover with the oil and warm very slowly over a low heat. When the oil is warm to the touch, move the saucepan over a pilot light until the tuna is opaque and flaky. (In the absence of a pilot light, periodically switch the heat on and off to maintain a temperature of 40–45°C/104–113°F until the tuna is cooked.)

Lift the cooked tuna out of the oil. Strain the remaining oil through muslin and discard the herbs and spices. Keep the recovered oil in a clean plastic container in the refrigerator.

Bring a small saucepan of water to the boil and gently lower in the eggs. Boil until the white is set and the yolk is still runny in the centre (6–6½ minutes). Refresh under cold running water. When cool enough to handle, shell the eggs.

Fry the lardons in a frying pan over a high heat, stirring occasionally. When crisp and browned, deglaze the pan with the balsamic vinegar and take off the heat. Squeeze in the lemon juice and whisk in the extra virgin olive oil.

Coarsely shred the tuna confit and divide between 4 small plates. Cut each boiled egg in half lengthways. Place 2 halves on each plate and spoon the pancetta dressing over everything. Garnish with a few crisp salad leaves.

Smoked mackerel pâté with burnt rolls

Serves 6–8

600ml (1 pint) double cream

700g (1lb 9oz) smoked mackerel fillets, skin removed

1 sheet of leaf gelatine, soaked in cold water until softened

salt and pepper

pinch of cayenne pepper

To serve

50g (1¾oz) cracked black pepper, blitzed in a spice mill or food processor

1 batch of Burnt rolls (*see* page 195)

100g (3½oz) unsalted butter

I have to confess, this wonderful recipe actually belongs to Nicci's Auntie Cathy, who is a brilliant cook and was a great inspiration to me when I was training, when Nicci and I would visit her family in Scotland at Christmas and enjoy her wonderful food.

Whisk the double cream into soft peaks.

Blitz the smoked mackerel in a food processor until smooth. Press the mackerel paste through a fine sieve with the back of a spoon into a metal bowl sitting on a bed of ice.

With the bowl still on ice, slowly beat in the cream a little at a time until only about 50ml (2fl oz) remains.

Gently heat the remaining cream to about 50°C (122°F) in a small saucepan. Drain the gelatine and stir into the hot cream until melted. Set aside to cool. When cold, beat the cream jelly into the fish paste and season with salt, pepper and cayenne.

Stack 4 pieces of clingfilm, each about the size of an A4 piece of paper, on a flat work surface.

Spoon the smoked mackerel pâté across the middle of the cling film and roll up to form a sausage shape. Twist the ends in opposite directions to form a tight cylinder, taking care not to trap any air inside. Cool the pâté in the refrigerator for about 3 hours until firm.

Unwrap the pâté and roll through the black pepper to form a fine dark crust. Slice into 6–8 pieces and serve with the burnt rolls and butter.

Octopus carpaccio with tomato salsa and basil

Serves 6

2 tbsp olive oil

3 garlic cloves, finely chopped

1 leek, cleaned and finely chopped

1 celery stick, finely chopped

1 small onion, finely chopped

1 large British octopus
(best in summer)

125ml (4fl oz) white wine

Tomato salsa

1 small red onion, finely chopped

1 sprig of tarragon

8 basil leaves

4 plum tomatoes, dunked in
boiling water for 3 seconds, then
skinned, deseeded and finely
chopped into neat squares

1 handful of flat leaf parsley
leaves, finely chopped

To serve

1 handful of rocket

1 lemon, cut into 6 wedges

2–3 tbsp extra virgin olive oil

I heard about this from an Italian guy who came to fix my coffee machine. He told me he missed his mamma's cooking, especially his favourite dish, Octopus Carpaccio. I got the gist of the recipe from him and it evolved into what you see here.

Heat the olive oil in a heavy-based saucepan over a low heat. Add the garlic and fry for 2–3 minutes. Then add the vegetables, cover and sweat for a further 15 minutes.

Meanwhile, rinse the octopus under the cold tap and snap the flap of skin connecting the hood to the body (inside the head behind the eyes). Turn the head inside out and remove the brains and innards. Slash behind the eyes and remove them.

Remove the vegetables from the saucepan and increase the heat. Put in the octopus with its beak down and tentacles draped over its head. Fry briefly, then pour in the wine. Return the vegetables to the saucepan, cover, then braise the octopus over a low heat for 1 hour. Uncover and set aside to cool.

Lay 5 sheets of clingfilm, a little bigger than an A4 sheet of paper, on top of each other on a flat work surface.

Remove the octopus from the saucepan and place on the clingfilm. Cut out the beak and cut gently between each tentacle, then wrap them around the head. Add some braising liquid to the octopus parcel, twist the ends of the clingfilm at the top, then tie tightly. Twist the beak end to form a tight round parcel with no air trapped inside. Refrigerate overnight.

Mix all the salsa ingredients together.

Remove the octopus from the refrigerator and slice it as thinly as possible using a sharp, thin-bladed knife, mandolin or meat slicer. The thinner the slices, the more tender it will be.

Arrange the slices on 6 plates and season with a sprinkling of salt and pepper. Place a pile of rocket on each plate and spoon the salsa on top. Serve with lemon wedges and a drizzle of extra virgin olive oil.

Smoked salmon with potato salad and homemade salad cream

Serves 4

200–300g (7–10½oz) smoked salmon
bunch of watercress, about 100g (3½oz)

Salad cream
1 tbsp plain flour
4 tsp caster sugar
1 tsp English mustard powder
pinch of salt
2 free-range eggs
100ml (3½fl oz) white wine vinegar
150ml (¼ pint) double cream
squeeze of lemon juice

Warm potato salad
1kg (1lb 2oz) new potatoes
4 tbsp extra virgin olive oil
4 tbsp capers
1 bunch of tarragon, leaves only, chopped
juice and rind of 1 unwaxed lemon
salt and pepper

Whether you want something light to offer at a barbecue or something to kick-start a dinner party, this is perfect. The familiar flavours are so good together: the creamy acidity of the homemade salad cream cuts through the smooth smokiness of the salmon and sparks up the new potatoes beautifully.

To make the salad cream, put the flour, sugar, mustard powder and salt in a mixing bowl and mix well. Beat the eggs and white wine vinegar together and stir into the dry ingredients.

Sit the mixing bowl over a saucepan of simmering water and stir for 5–6 minutes until warmed and thickened. Remove from the heat and set aside to cool.

Fold the cream through the mixture and add the lemon juice. The salad cream is now ready and can be kept in the refrigerator for 1–2 weeks.

To prepare the potato salad, bring a large saucepan of lightly salted cold water to the boil. Drop in the potatoes and cook until a small sharp pointed knife spears a potato with ease.

Strain the potatoes into a colander. Transfer to a large mixing bowl and crush each one between your thumb and fingers or, if too hot, with the back of a spoon, to give the dressing more chance to flavour the potatoes.

Add the olive oil, capers, tarragon, lemon juice and rind and salt and pepper to taste. Toss well to blend the flavours.

To serve, either arrange the watercress on a large serving platter and tip the potato salad on top, or divide the watercress between 4 separate plates and top with the potato salad. Lay the slices of smoked salmon over the potatoes and finish with spoonfuls of the salad cream.

Crostini misti

A selection of toasted thinly sliced ciabatta bread with marinated meat, fish, vegetables or cheese toppings, crostini are great as party canapés, or for snacking on through a movie.

1 ciabatta loaf
1 garlic clove, cut in half
extra virgin olive oil for drizzling

To make the *crostini*, cut the bread into 3mm (⅛ in) slices and grill on a griddle pan or toast under a grill until branded with clear bar marks. When golden brown, rub the cut face of the garlic over the toasted slices and drizzle over some olive oil.

Here are some of my favourite toppings:

Black olive tapenade

Makes 125ml (4fl oz)

1 tsp finely chopped shallot
½ garlic clove, pressed
100g (3½oz) taggiasca olives, pitted and roughly chopped
1 tbsp capers, coarsely chopped
1 tbsp white wine vinegar
juice of ½ lemon
1 tbsp finely chopped flat leaf parsley leaves
½ tbsp finely chopped parsley stalks
1 tbsp finely chopped celery leaves
5 tbsp extra virgin olive oil
salt and pepper

Stir all the ingredients together in a mixing bowl and spread over the *crostini*.

Garden peas, Pecorino, mint and crispy pancetta

Serves 4

100g (3½oz) garden peas, fresh or frozen, cooked
50g (1¾oz) Pecorino, grated
6 mint leaves
1 tbsp extra virgin olive oil
salt and pepper
4 slices pancetta or streaky bacon, grilled until crisp

Toss the peas, Pecorino, mint, olive oil, salt and pepper together in a mixing bowl, then mash together with a fork to crush the peas. Spread over the *crostini* and finish with a slice of pancetta.

Mozzarella, sun-blushed tomatoes and basil

Serves 4

1 ball of mozzarella
3 sun-blushed tomatoes
4 basil leaves
1 tsp extra virgin olive oil
sea salt crystals and cracked black pepper

Roughly chop the ingredients, mix together in a bowl and spread over 4 *crostini*.

Simple tomato salad with basil and grissini

Serves 4–6

200g (7oz) Basic bread dough
(*see* page 178)
50g (1¾oz) durum wheat semolina
1 tbsp olive oil

Tomato salad

500g (1lb 2oz) mixed tomatoes, the
freshest and tastiest available
1 tbsp red wine vinegar
cracked black pepper
sea salt crystals
splash of extra virgin olive oil

To serve

extra virgin olive oil
1 bunch of fresh basil, leaves only
85g (3oz) *Parmigiano Reggiano*
cheese (optional)
aged balsamic vinegar (optional)

There are so many amazing tomatoes around these days, you don't have to settle for the bog-standard issue in the supermarkets any more. If you're turned on by tomatoes, get out there and look for some of the more unusual ones, such as red or yellow teardrops, mini plums, creamy-coloured cherries or black tomatoes, in your local farmers' markets or the wholesale vegetable markets.

Preheat the oven to 220°C/425°F/gas mark 7. Line a baking sheet with baking paper.

To make the grissini, roll out the proved dough into a long sausage-shape under your fingers. Cut into 8 equal pieces and roll each to the thickness of a pencil. Roll in the semolina.

Arrange the breadsticks on the baking sheet and drizzle over the olive oil. Bake for 15 minutes then switch off the oven, leaving the breadsticks inside to cool.

Cut the smaller tomatoes in half and the larger ones into 5mm (½in) slices or wedges. Put all the tomatoes in a bowl, season well and stir in the red wine vinegar and pepper.

To serve, divide the tomatoes between 4–6 plates. Drizzle a little extra virgin olive oil around the plate and garnish with the basil leaves. Shave *Parmigiano Reggiano* over the top and drizzle over a little balsamic vinegar if you like. Serve immediately with the grissini.

Mixed grilled vegetables

The Italians know this fantastic dish as verdura mista. I always look forward to summer when all these lovely vegetables are in season and super fresh. They're gorgeous, whether you serve them on their own or with some spring lamb and a beautiful herb dressing, such as salsa verde or fresh mint sauce.

Serves 4

75ml (2½ fl oz) extra virgin olive oil

juice and rind of 1 unwaxed lemon

salt and pepper

2 red onions, cut into 8 wedges

2 red peppers, cored, deseeded and quartered

4 artichoke hearts, finely sliced

1 aubergine cut into 1cm (½ in) slices

1 courgette, cut into 5mm (¼ in) slices

1 bunch of mint, leaves only, roughly chopped

Heat a griddle pan until very hot. Preheat the oven to 180°C/350°F/gas mark 4.

Put 50ml (2fl oz) of the olive oil and the lemon rind and juice in a large roasting tin. Sprinkle over a generous pinch of salt and pepper and set aside.

Toss all the vegetables in the remaining olive oil in a large bowl. Grill the onions and peppers on the hot griddle until clear dark bar marks are visible (about 5 minutes). Transfer to the roasting tin. Grill the artichokes, aubergines and courgettes and add to the roasting tin.

Roast the vegetables until the edges are slightly charred (about 30 minutes). Remove from the oven and toss in the chopped mint.

Serve as a vegetarian dish or with roast chicken or grilled salmon.

Shaved fennel, apple and Pecorino Sardo salad

I first came across this salad when my friend Andy came back from Italy and put it on the menu in the trattoria at Fifteen. Crisp sweet apple and crunchy aniseed-flavoured fennel with some Pecorino shavings make a wonderfully refreshing salad. I'll let you into a little secret: it's best to use Pink Lady apples and Florence fennel here.

Serves 4

½ head of radicchio, core removed
1 Florence fennel bulb, tough outer leaves removed,
stalks trimmed from the top and any green fronds reserved
1 Pink Lady apple
juice of ½ lemon
100g (3½oz) Pecorino Sardo (or Fiore Sardo with red chilli)
70g (2½oz) rocket
salt and pepper

Vinaigrette
3 tbsp olive oil
4 tsp lemon juice
salt and pepper

Gently wash the radicchio leaves. Shake lightly in a colander and set aside to drain.

Cut the fennel bulb in half from top to bottom and slice as thinly as possible. (A mandolin is ideal for doing this.) Cut the apple into 4, carefully remove the core and pips and slice very thinly. (Again, a mandolin is useful here.) Gently toss the apple slices in the lemon juice to stop them browning.

Use a potato peeler to shave the Pecorino into a bowl.

For the vinaigrette, whisk together the oil and lemon juice and season to taste.

When ready to serve, gently toss the radicchio and rocket leaves with the shaved fennel, fennel fronds and apple slices in the vinaigrette. Season and scatter the Pecorino flakes on top. To avoid crushing the leaves, very carefully lift the salad into 4 bowls. Serve immediately as the dressed leaves will brown if left too long.

Funky leaf salad

Funky leaf salad is a good all-rounder: you can use any and as many leaves as you fancy. The beauty of salads like this is that you can dress them with whatever you like to suit the occasion. My favourite has to be loads of chicory leaves with a lemon and pomegranate dressing to serve with roasted duck breast.

Serves 4–6

1 head of radicchio, outer leaves discarded
1 head of chicory, outer leaves discarded
1 head of dandelion leaves
1 handful of rocket
1 bunch of tarragon, leaves only
1 bunch of basil, leaves only
1 bunch of mint, leaves only
4 tbsp capers
salt and pepper
juice of 1 lemon
4 tbsp extra virgin olive oil

To serve
100g (3½oz) *Parmigiano Reggiano* cheese
aged balsamic vinegar for drizzling

Tear the inner leaves from the radicchio and chicory into a sink of clean cold water. Add the dandelion leaves and rocket. Wash thoroughly but gently, because the leaves bruise easily.

Drain the leaves and pile on to a clean tea towel to dry.

Tip the salad leaves into a large salad bowl along with the tarragon, basil, mint, capers and salt and pepper. Sprinkle over the lemon juice and olive oil and toss well. Finish with some shavings of *Parmigiano Reggiano* and a drizzle of aged balsamic vinegar.

bread

Bread was the first thing that I ever cooked. My dad would often make bread at home when money was hard to come by. He would always put the dough in the airing cupboard to prove as it was one of the warmest places in the house. I wasn't interested in baking at the time, but my passion for it grew while I was working at Fifteen.

At Fifteen we worked with a baker called John. We would start baking at midnight and work through to seven in the morning, making all kinds of breads. It was great. There's something really special about creating a tasty and humble loaf just from flour, water and yeast.

The secret to making great bread is to be patient; it's essential to prove the bread dough at least twice before baking to ensure you end up with a light and fluffy loaf. Another tip is to weigh the water used in the recipe rather than measure it in a measuring jug, as this is a more accurate form of measurement.

Basic bread dough

Bread is one of the oldest prepared foods, dating back to prehistoric times. The bread-making technique is as simple now as it has always been, the key ingredients being flour and water. Leavened bread, made with yeast, probably first came about when bread dough came into contact with the natural bacteria in the atmosphere. Basic bread is so simple to make – why not have a go at this recipe?

Makes 2 loaves

20g (¾oz) caster sugar

700ml (1¼pints) tepid water, plus more as required

20g (¾oz) fresh yeast (available from some bakeries, bakery sections in supermarkets and health food stores)

1kg (2lb 4oz) strong white bread flour, plus extra for dusting

20g (¾oz) salt

1. Line a baking tray with baking paper.

2. Dissolve the sugar in the water. Crumble in the yeast and whisk until evenly dispersed. Set aside in a warm place until the liquid is frothing (about 15 minutes).

3. Sift the flour and salt into a large mixing bowl and make a well in the middle. Pour in the yeast water and work into the flour to form a ball of pliable dough. Add a little more warm water, if needed, to get the right consistency.

4. On a lightly floured work surface, knead the dough until smooth and springy (about 5 minutes). Put the dough back in the bowl, cover with clingfilm and set aside to rise in a warm, draught-free place for 1 hour.

5. When the dough has nearly doubled in size, turn it out on to a lightly floured work surface. Divide in half and shape each piece into a loaf. Place the loaves well apart on the baking sheet. With a sharp knife, cut 3 slashes, about 1cm (½in) deep, in the top of both loaves. Cover with a cloth and set aside in a warm place to prove for another hour. Preheat the oven to 220°C/425°F/gas mark 7.

6. Bake the bread until browned and crusty (about 25 minutes). Set the loaves aside on a wire rack to cool for 30 minutes before slicing.

Fennel and polenta bread

I can remember exactly where and when I first hit on this recipe: I was training at Fifteen at the time. It must have been about 3am and I was on the bakery shift with John the baker. He always encouraged us to come up with our own ideas for flavouring the dough. I wanted to make a bread that went well with fish, so fennel seeds came into my head. And because John used lots of semolina in his breads and I wanted to keep an Italian feel to my bread, I decided to use polenta. It turned out to be a fantastic combination. I still bake lots of fennel and polenta bread – and so does John.

Serves 4

1 batch of Basic bread dough (*see* page 178)
200g (7oz) polenta plus extra for dusting
60g (2 ¼ oz) fennel seeds, lightly toasted in a dry frying pan
50ml (2fl oz) extra virgin olive oil
sea salt crystals

Make up the basic bread dough, using 800g (1lb 12oz) strong bread flour and 200g (7oz) polenta. Add the fennel seeds to the dry ingredients before mixing.

The polenta dough is quite dense so let it rise in a wide bowl where it can spread out rather than up. Cover with clingfilm and set aside in a warm place to rise for 1 hour.

Turn the risen dough out on to a lightly floured work surface and tear in half. Shape each piece into a loaf, use a sharp knife to slash the tops with diagonal lines, and brush with olive oil. Dust with polenta and set aside in a warm place to prove for a further hour. Preheat the oven to 200°C/400°F/gas mark 6.

Line 2 baking sheets with baking paper and place 1 fennel and polenta loaf on each. Sprinkle some sea salt on top and bake for 25 minutes. Set aside to cool on a wire rack before slicing.

Rosemary and raisin bread

This bread is excellent served with a cheese board as the raisins are a great complement to cheese. I soak the raisins in Vin Santo wine for several hours before use to flavour and soften them. This stops them from splitting the dough. Make sure you shape the bread tightly so that it is long and thin with an even crumb inside.

Makes 2 loaves

400g (14oz) Basic bread dough (*see* page 178)
100g (3½oz) raisins soaked in 2 tbsp Vin Santo and 1 tbsp white wine
2 sprigs of rosemary, leaves only
salt

When making the basic bread dough, in step 3 drain the soaked raisins and knead into the dough with the rosemary until both are evenly distributed.

With well-floured hands, tear the dough in half and shape each piece into a loaf. Alternatively, break the dough into smaller pieces to form rolls (*see* picture, opposite). Use your thumbs to fold the dough in half and pinch the fold tightly shut between thumb and forefinger. Repeat the folding and pinching twice to create a neat loaf.

Line a baking sheet with baking paper and space the loaves well apart on top. Make 5 slashes across the top of each loaf and set aside in a warm place to prove until well risen (45–50 minutes).

Preheat the oven to 220°C/425°F/gas mark 7.

Bake the loaves or rolls until browned and crusty (25 minutes for loaves, 20 minutes for rolls). Switch off the oven and leave the bread to cool inside for 10 minutes. Transfer to a wire rack to finish cooling.

Turmeric flatbreads

Makes 6

1 tbsp turmeric

250g (9oz) strong white flour, plus extra for dusting

1 tsp salt

125g (4oz) water

These are similar to West Indian rotis, except they're grilled rather than fried. Flatbreads are easier to make than leavened bread as they contain no yeast.

Mix all the ingredients together in a mixing bowl to make a soft dough.

Tear the dough into 6 even pieces. Lightly flour a work surface and roll out each piece with a rolling pin to a long flatbread about 3mm (⅛in) thick.

Grill the flatbreads straightaway on a barbecue or hot griddle pan for 20 seconds on each side.

Tomato bread cones

Makes about 20 cones

1 batch of Basic bread dough (*see* page 178)

500g (1lb 2oz) cherry tomatoes

1 garlic clove, finely chopped

150ml (5fl oz) extra virgin olive oil

salt and pepper

1 handful of basil leaves

flour for dusting

These bread cones are a great start to a meal and can be filled with your favourite choice of meat and vegetables.

Make the basic bread dough up to and including point 4. Cover and set aside in a warm place to rise for 1 hour.

While the dough is rising, put the tomatoes, garlic and 4 tbsp of the olive oil into a saucepan and stew for 15 minutes over a medium heat. Stir in salt and pepper to taste. Set aside to cool.

When risen, roll the dough out on a lightly floured work surface with a rolling pin to a sheet about 5mm (¼in) thick and cut into 15cm (6in) squares.

Preheat the oven to 200°C/400°F/gas mark 6. Line 2 baking sheets with baking paper.

Put 1 tbsp of the tomatoes in the centre of a square of dough with a few basil leaves and roll into a cone shape.

Brush olive oil over the cones and arrange on the baking sheets. Set aside in a warm place to prove for a further hour.

Bake until browned (25 minutes), turning occasionally.

Lavosh (Armenian flatbread)

Makes lots

1kg (2lb 4oz) strong bread flour plus extra for dusting

1½ tsp salt

1 tsp caster sugar

2 tbsp poppy seeds

2 tbsp sesame seeds

1 tbsp turmeric

1 tbsp chilli powder (optional)

1 free-range egg, lightly beaten

200ml (7fl oz) milk at room temperature

500g (1lb 2oz) butter, melted and cooled

Lavosh is one of the oldest breads that exists. It's highly likely that southern Italians came into contact with this Middle-Eastern flatbread as a result of salt trading. Serve with pâté, salsa or cream cheese.

Preheat the oven to 180°C/350°F/gas mark 4. Line 2 baking sheets with baking paper.

Mix together the flour, salt, sugar, poppy seeds, sesame seeds, turmeric and, if you like, chilli powder in a large mixing bowl.

In a separate bowl, whisk together the egg, milk and melted butter. Make a well in the centre of the dry ingredients, pour in the liquid and work it vigorously into the flour to form a smooth dough.

Tear the dough into 4 equal pieces. Roll out into sheets as thin as a pancake. Prick with a fork to stop the dough puffing up during baking. Cut each sheet into triangles the size of tortilla chips.

Arrange as many dough triangles as possible on the baking sheets, leaving a little gap between each. Bake until crisp and browned (10–15 minutes). Repeat until all the dough triangles are baked.

Ciabatta bread

Makes 4 loaves

450g (1lb) tipo '00' flour, plus extra
for dusting
1 tbsp fast-action dried yeast
1 tbsp salt
350g (12oz) warm water
50ml (2fl oz) olive oil, plus extra
for brushing over the loaves

The ferment (starter dough)
350g (12oz) tipo '00' flour
175ml (6fl oz) warm water
1 tsp fast-action dried yeast

Ciabatta is the most difficult and time consuming of all the breads I make. Treat it like a baby – with care and love – to achieve the best results. Large air bubbles give ciabatta its characteristic holes. Don't shape ciabatta as you would other breads – this can burst the air bubbles and spoil the loaf.

To make the ferment, mix all the ingredients together in a large mixing bowl to form a soft dough. Cover with a damp cloth and set aside at room temperature for 24 hours.

The following day, line 2 baking sheets with baking paper.

To make the rolls, mix the flour, yeast and salt together in a large mixing bowl. Then add the ferment, water and olive oil. Mix thoroughly until the dough comes away cleanly from the side of the bowl.

Tip the dough out on to a lightly floured work surface and knead until smooth and springy (at least 10 minutes). Oil a mixing bowl and put in the dough. Cover with clingfilm and set aside in a warm place to rise for 1 hour.

When the dough has almost doubled in volume, tip it out on to a floured work surface and cut into 4 pieces with a scraper or plastic spatula. Gently pull out these 4 lumps of dough into long slipper shapes (*see* left), taking care to knock out as little air as possible. Turn the loaves over to dust the tops with flour. Place the right way up on the baking sheets. Set aside to prove for a further hour.

Preheat the oven to 220°C/425°F/ gas mark 7.

Meanwhile, place a roasting tin half full of hot water in the bottom of the oven. To fill the oven with steam, give the tin a little shake as the bread goes in to bake. (The steam will stop the crusts on the loaves cracking.)

Bake until browned (17–20 minutes). Turn off the oven and transfer the loaves from the baking sheets directly on to the oven shelves. Leave to cool inside.

Ferment (starter dough)

Before making sourdough, you have to prepare the ferment (starter dough), which takes 5 days.

DAY ONE

Morning

50ml (2fl oz) tepid water

25g (1oz) rye flour

Evening

50ml (2fl oz) tepid water

25g (1oz) rye flour

Put the water into a 700ml (1¼ pint) pickling jar, stir in the flour, seal the lid and leave in a warm place (around 25°C/77°F) for 24 hours. Do this once in the morning and once in the evening.

DAY TWO

Morning

50ml (2fl oz) tepid water

25g (1oz) rye flour

Evening

50ml (2fl oz) tepid water

25g (1oz) rye flour

Add the water to the ferment from day one then stir in the flour. Seal and store in a warm place (around 25°C/77°F) for 24 hours. Do this once in the morning and once in the evening.

DAY THREE

Morning

50ml (2fl oz) tepid water

25g (1oz) rye flour

Evening

50ml (2fl oz) tepid water

25g (1oz) rye flour

Add the water to the ferment from day two and then stir in the flour. Seal and store in a warm place (around 25°C/77°F) for 24 hours. Do this once in the morning and once in the evening.

DAY FOUR

Morning

50ml (2fl oz) tepid water

25g (1oz) rye flour

Evening

50ml (2fl oz) tepid water

25g (1oz) rye flour

Add the water to the ferment from day three and then stir in the flour. Cappuccino-style froth should have begun to develop in the ferment. Seal and store in a warm place (around 25°C/77°F) for 24 hours. Do this once in the morning and once in the evening.

DAY FIVE

100ml (3½ fl oz) tepid water

80g (3oz) rye flour

Discard four-fifths of the ferment from day four, then stir in day five's ingredients. Seal again and store in a warm place (around 25°C/77°F) for 24 hours.

NOTE When you have completed day five take out 400g (14oz) of the ferment for the sourdough recipe, then continue feeding the ferment by repeating this recipe.

Rye sourdough bread

Makes 2 loaves

300g (10½oz) strong white flour

500g (1lb 2oz) rye flour,
plus extra for dusting

25g (1oz) salt

400g (14oz) ferment
(starter dough)

600g (1lb 5oz) water

durum wheat semolina for dusting

Sourdough is a very dense bread with an even crumb and a nutty flavour. For the best results, prove the dough at least three times before shaping it, then one last time before baking. Sourdough bread is wonderful toasted and served with warm cannellini beans and loads of good extra virgin olive oil.

Mix the flours and salt in a large mixing bowl and make a well in the centre. Add the ferment and a little of the water, then slowly work in the flour with a wooden spoon. Pour in the remaining water and mix well until a soft dough comes cleanly away from the side of the bowl. Turn out on to a work surface lightly dusted with rye flour and knead for 10–15 minutes.

Transfer the dough to a large mixing bowl, cover with a damp cloth and set aside in a warm place to rise for 1½ hours.

Cut the dough into 2 pieces and gently shape both into square lumps of dough. Cover with a damp cloth and leave to prove for another hour.

Work on 1 piece of dough at a time. Place on a work surface dusted with semolina and fold the bottom and top edges to the centre, then pinch the two edges firmly together, effectively folding the dough in half. Then fold the top edge over to the bottom edge, pinching the seam together and forming the dough into a sausage shape. Press your thumbs into the seam and lift the far side of the dough towards you to form a neat cylindrical loaf. Pinch the new seam together again to seal tightly. Repeat with the second square of dough.

Place the 2 loaves, seam sides down, on 2 baking sheets lined with baking paper. Cover with a damp cloth and set aside in a warm place to prove for a further 45 minutes.

Meanwhile, preheat the oven to 220°C/425°F/gas mark 7.

Slash the top of each loaf 5 times with a sharp knife. Put a roasting tin half full of hot water in the bottom of the oven. (The steam will stop the crusts on the loaves cracking.) Bake the loaves for 25–30 minutes, then cool on a wire rack.

Grissini

Makes 20

400g (14oz) Basic bread dough
(*see* page 178)

100g (3½ oz) durum wheat
semolina

2 tbsp olive oil

Grissini are served everywhere in Italy – in wineries,
restaurants, bars and even people's homes. The semolina
in this recipe makes the bread crisp and crunchy.

Preheat the oven to 220°C/425°F/gas mark 7.

After proving, roll the dough into a very long sausage-shape.
Cut into 20 equal pieces and roll under your fingers to the
thickness of a pencil. Roll in the semolina to coat. Place on a
baking sheet lined with baking paper and drizzle with olive oil.

Bake for 15 minutes then switch off the oven, leaving the
breadsticks inside to cool.

Mini focaccia

Makes 1 large loaf

500g (1lb 2oz) strong bread flour, plus extra for dusting

15g (½oz) fast-action dried yeast

2 tsp salt

300ml (½ pint) warm water

50ml (2fl oz) olive oil, plus extra for brushing over the loaf

1 tbsp clear honey mixed with 1 tbsp warm water

4 sprigs of rosemary, leaves only

large pinch of sea salt crystals

Focaccia is an airy, fluffy Italian bread, which is traditionally topped with rosemary, extra virgin olive oil and sea salt. It is eaten at the table in Italy, usually served with olive oil and balsamic vinegar, or perhaps even some tapenade (olive pâté).

Mix the flour, yeast and salt together in a large mixing bowl. Stir in the water and olive oil and mix thoroughly until the dough comes away cleanly from the side of the bowl.

Tip the dough out on to a lightly floured work surface and knead until smooth and springy (at least 10 minutes). Oil a mixing bowl and put in the dough. Cover with a cloth and set aside in a warm place to rise for 1 hour.

When the dough has almost doubled in volume, tip it on to a baking sheet lined with baking paper and spread it into a thick slab with your fingertips. Cover with a cloth and set aside in a warm place to prove for a further 30 minutes.

Meanwhile, preheat the oven to 230°C/450°F/gas mark 8. Place a roasting tin half full of hot water in the bottom of the oven. To fill the oven with steam, give the tin a little shake as the bread goes in to bake. (The steam will stop the crusts on the loaves cracking.)

When the dough has risen again, brush the top of the loaf with the thinned honey and press in the rosemary, using your fingertips to make little pits all over the surface. Brush the loaf all over with olive oil and sprinkle over the salt crystals.

As soon as the loaf goes in the oven, turn the temperature down to 220°C/425°F/gas mark 7 and bake for 25–30 minutes.

Burnt rolls

Makes 32 rolls

450g (1lb) tipo '00' flour, plus extra
for dusting

1 tbsp fast-action dried yeast

1 tbsp salt

350g (12oz) warm water

50ml (2fl oz) olive oil, plus extra
for finishing

1 tbsp clear honey mixed with
1 tbsp warm water

The ferment (starter dough)

350g (12oz) tipo '00' flour

1 tsp fast-action dried yeast

175ml (6fl oz) warm water

These rolls are most deliciously moreish. To ensure a crispy shell and a hollow fluffy centre, make sure your dough is light and airy. Brush a little watered-down honey on top before the rolls go in the oven to help them burn.

To make the ferment, mix all the ingredients together in a large mixing bowl to form a soft dough. Cover with a cloth and set aside at room temperature for 24 hours.

The following day, line 2 baking sheets with baking paper.

To make the rolls, mix the flour, yeast and salt together in a large mixing bowl. Then add the ferment, water and olive oil. Mix thoroughly until the dough comes away cleanly from the side of the bowl.

Tip the dough out on to a lightly floured work surface and knead for at least 10 minutes. Shape the dough into a ball and put in an oiled mixing bowl. Cover with a cloth and set aside in a warm place to rise for 1 hour.

When the dough has almost doubled in volume, tip it on to a lightly floured work surface. Cut into 32 little pieces and shape into balls between your palms. Arrange the dough balls on the 2 baking sheets, spacing them well apart. Set aside in a warm place to prove for a further hour.

Meanwhile, preheat the oven to 230°C/450°F/gas mark 8. Place a roasting tin half full of hot water in the bottom of the oven. To fill the oven with steam, give the tin a little shake as the bread goes in to bake. The steam will prevent the crusts on the rolls cracking.

After proving, brush the tops of the dough balls with the diluted honey. Bake for 10 minutes, then switch the top and bottom baking sheets around to ensure an even colour on all the rolls. (There's less need to do this if you have a fan oven with a uniform temperature throughout.) Continue baking until the rolls are quite dark and shiny on top but soft in the centre. Leave to cool a little before serving warm.

desserts

This chapter contains some of my favourite desserts. They're all really easy to make as long as you follow the recipe closely. The beauty of desserts is that they can be as easy or as complicated as you like. Italian cooking is all about simplicity, and my favourite dessert is just a bang-in-season peach torn open and served with cream – it's fresh, juicy, sweet and moreish.

If you're having a dinner party with friends, choose something simple – you don't want to be stuck in the kitchen while everyone else is drinking wine and having fun. My Amalfi lemon curd tart is a great option as you can make it in advance and leave it to set in the fridge until you need to serve it. Alternatively, if you want something hot, why not try my Apple crumble with honey mascarpone – then your guests can help themselves at the table. Whatever you decide on, remember to keep it seasonal and to have fun!

Amalfi lemon curd tart

Serves 12

Sweet pastry
(for 1 x 25cm/10in tart shell)
250g (9oz) plain flour
100g (3½oz) icing sugar
pinch of salt
100g (3½oz) unsalted butter, cubed
2 large free-range eggs, at room temperature, beaten

Lemon filling
7 whole free-range eggs
7 free-range egg yolks
(save the whites for making Meringue with summer berries, *see* page 217)
300ml (½ pint) fresh lemon juice
rind of 2 unwaxed Amalfi lemons
280g (10oz) caster sugar
325g (11½oz) butter, cubed

Chantilly cream
175ml (6fl oz) double cream
1 vanilla pod
25g (1oz) icing sugar, or to taste

To decorate
icing sugar for dusting
juice and finely grated rind of 1 unwaxed Amalfi lemon

This will be the best lemon tart you will ever indulge in – providing you use the right lemons. The rinds of unwaxed Amalfi lemons are sweeter than those of standard lemons, especially as they are exposed to the Mediterranean sunshine. In some parts of Amalfi the lemons are baked and eaten whole! Buy them at any good market that imports Italian produce.

For the sweet pastry, sieve the flour, icing sugar and salt on to a clean work surface. Rub the butter into the dry ingredients with your fingertips until the mixture resembles breadcrumbs. Make a well in the centre and add the eggs. Draw in the flour from the edges and work the mixture together to give a consistent dough. Flour the work surface and knead the dough 3–4 times. Don't overwork the pastry. Now flatten the pastry, wrap it in clingfilm and rest it in the refrigerator for at least an hour.

Remove the rested sweet pastry from the refrigerator and set aside for 10 minutes to reach room temperature. With a rolling pin, roll out the sweet pastry on to a large sheet of clingfilm or baking paper into a very thin round, about 30cm (12in) across. Wind the clingfilm-pastry sheet on to the rolling pin. Use to line a 25cm (10in) loose-bottomed fluted tart tin.

Peel off the clingfilm and roll the rolling pin over the top of the tart tin to trim off any excess pastry. Prick the base with a fork and return to the refrigerator to firm up for 10–15 minutes.

Preheat the oven to 190°C/375°F/gas mark 5.

Line the pastry base with enough baking paper to rise above the side of the tin by 20cm (8in) all the way around. Fill the case to above the rim of the tin with either lentils or small dried beans. Bake for 10 minutes, then carefully lift out the baking paper with the beans and store to use again. Return the pastry case to the oven until cooked through and sandy brown (about 4 more minutes).

To make the filling, put all the ingredients, apart from the butter, in a large stainless steel saucepan. Place over a low heat and whisk continuously until the liquid starts to foam. Continue whisking as the foam is reabsorbed while the lemon

curd thickens. Reduce the heat to minimum and gradually drop in the butter. Whisk briskly for another 5 minutes until melted.

Put the cooked pastry case on a flat, level surface and carefully pour the lemon curd into the centre. Gently tap the tin occasionally to help the filling settle. Fill right to the top but take care, as there may be more lemon curd than the case can hold. Store any leftover lemon curd in the refrigerator.

Set aside to cool. The texture of the pastry case and flavour of the filling are better if the tart isn't refrigerated.

While the tart is cooling, prepare the Chantilly cream. Pour the cream into a bowl and scrape in the vanilla seeds. Add the icing sugar and whisk together to form stiff peaks.

To decorate the tart, either lightly dust the top with icing sugar or give it a caramel glaze. For the glaze, sift a thick coating of icing sugar over the tart and blast with a blowtorch for a shiny, crisp, caramelized finish.

Serve with a neat scoop of Chantilly cream, a drizzle of lemon juice and a sprinkling of lemon rind.

Lemon and polenta cake

Serves 12

450g (1lb) unsalted butter, softened

plain flour for dusting

450g (1lb) caster sugar

450g (1lb) ground almonds

2 tsp vanilla extract

6 free-range eggs

rind of 4 unwaxed lemons, juice of 1

225g (8oz) polenta

¼ tsp salt

Full of flavour and texture, this delightful cake can be enjoyed on any occasion. I always use the best ingredients available, especially when a recipe is so simple. Unwaxed Amalfi lemons are the ideal choice as they're full of flavour and there are no chemicals on the skin.

Preheat the oven to 170°C/325°F/gas mark 3.

Butter and flour a 23cm (9in) round cake tin.

Beat the butter and sugar together until pale and light. Then stir in the ground almonds and vanilla extract.

Beat in the eggs, one at a time, working each egg into the mixture before adding the next.

Fold in the lemon rind and juice, followed by the polenta and salt. Spoon the mixture into the cake tin and level out the top with a spatula.

Bake in the oven for 1 hour 30–1 hour 50 minutes or until a fine skewer inserted into the centre of the cake comes out without any cake mixture sticking to it and the cake is cooked.

Leave to cool in the cake tin for 10 minutes before turning out on to a wire rack to finish cooling.

Raspberry frangipane tart

**Serves 8 for afternoon tea
or 12 as a dessert**

1 batch of sweet pastry
(*see* page 200)

Chantilly cream (*see* page 200),
pouring cream or vanilla ice
cream, to serve

Almond filling

350g (12oz) flaked almonds

350g (12oz) caster sugar

350g (12oz) unsalted butter,
softened

2 large free-range eggs

Raspberry topping

100g (3½oz) good-quality
raspberry jam

450g (1lb) raspberries

This tart can be served either warm or chilled. It is simple
to make and extremely versatile, as the flavours can be
varied according to your taste. You can bake it with dry fruit
but it works best with fresh fruits as their natural sugars and
moisture penetrate the tart, giving it great texture and
delicious flavour.

Preheat the oven to 190°C/375°F/gas mark 5.

Line the tart tin with the pastry, baking paper and beans as
described in the Amalfi lemon curd tart recipe (*see* page 200).
Blind bake the pastry case for just 6 minutes, then remove the
baking paper and beans and bake for another 4 minutes. Let
the pastry case cool and firm up for about 10 minutes. Turn
the oven down to 170°C/325°F/gas mark 3.

Meanwhile, put the almonds and caster sugar in a food
processor and blitz until the almonds are finely chopped.
Add the butter and blend into the dry ingredients. Then
pulse in the eggs.

Put the tart tin on a large baking sheet. Use a spatula to
transfer the almond mixture to the pastry case and spread it
evenly over the base.

Spoon small dollops of raspberry jam on to the almond filling.

Make sure the oven temperature has cooled down sufficiently
before placing the tart in the oven to bake for 40 minutes.
Every 10 minutes, check that the filling isn't rising too
dramatically. If it starts puffing up, leave the oven door open
for 1–2 minutes to let the heat escape before closing it again.

When the top is golden brown, remove the tart from the oven.
Cool to room temperature before covering the top with fresh
raspberries. Leave a 5mm (¼in) border uncovered around
the edge.

Serve slices of the raspberry frangipane tart with Chantilly
cream (*see* page 200), pouring cream or ice cream.

Chocolate fondant-soufflé

Chocolate fondant is a favourite with the ladies: the perfect choice for any fella who wants to impress his missis. Watch out, though – when you've cooked it once you'll be making it all the time! It's particularly good served with vanilla ice cream. Remember to butter the rim of the mould to enable the fondant to rise evenly.

Serves 6

3 tbsp cocoa powder, plus extra for dusting the moulds

100g (3½oz) good-quality chocolate (70 per cent cocoa solids), broken into small pieces

115g (4oz) unsalted butter

3 free-range eggs, separated into yolks and whites

140g (5oz) caster sugar

icing sugar for dusting

vanilla ice cream, to serve (optional)

Place 6 x 125ml (4fl oz) ovenproof moulds or cups in a refrigerator to cool. Preheat the oven to 200°C/400°F/gas mark 6.

Put the cocoa, chocolate and 90g (3¼oz) of the butter in a bowl sitting over a saucepan of simmering water. Make sure the bowl does not touch the water.

While the chocolate is melting, whisk the egg yolks and sugar together in a bowl until runny. Have a clean bowl and a whisk ready to whisk the egg whites.

Stir the melted chocolate into the sweetened egg yolks. Set aside in a warm place.

Take the moulds out of the refrigerator. Melt the remaining butter and use a pastry brush to butter the insides of the moulds. Brush with straight strokes up the sides and over the rims. Dust the buttered moulds with cocoa powder, tapping out any excess on to a sheet of baking paper.

Whisk the egg whites to stiff peaks. When stiff enough, you should be able to turn the bowl upside down without the froth falling out. Whisk a spoonful of the whites into the chocolate mixture, then very gently fold in the rest.

Spoon the fluffy chocolate mixture into a large piping bag or a strong plastic sandwich bag with one corner cut off and fill the moulds. Scrape the tops level using the back of a knife, taking care not to rub off any butter from the rims.

Place the moulds on a baking sheet and bake until risen (about 10 minutes). Dust with icing sugar and serve immediately, with scoops of vanilla ice cream, if you like.

Arborio rice pudding with rhubarb

Serves 6

600ml (1 pint) whole milk

250ml (9fl oz) double cream

40g (1½oz) sugar, plus extra
if needed

1 vanilla pod

300g (10½oz) Arborio rice

40g (1½oz) unsalted butter

Rhubarb

500ml (18fl oz) water

400g (14oz) caster sugar

350g (12oz) rhubarb, peeled (chop
and keep the peel) and cut into
5cm (2in) lengths

1 vanilla pod

Arborio rice is just one of many short-grained varieties on offer for cooking risottos and rice puddings. It's my favourite for puddings because the grains are a bit thicker than, say, carnaroli, so they tend to absorb more liquid and become more succulent and creamy.

To cook the rhubarb, pour the water and sugar into a heavy-based saucepan. Bring to the boil and add the rhubarb peel. Scrape in the vanilla seeds and reduce the heat.

Put the rhubarb in a frying basket and lower into the syrup. Simmer until the rhubarb is soft (about 5 minutes). Remove from the heat and set aside to cool.

To make the rice pudding, pour the milk, cream and sugar into a saucepan. Scrape in the vanilla seeds and bring to a simmer over a medium heat.

Tip the rice into another large heavy-based saucepan. Place over a moderate heat, stirring continuously with a wooden spoon, until the rice smells toasted.

Stir in a ladle of the hot milk immediately. As the liquid is absorbed, add another ladle, stirring all the time. Continue adding the milk, ladle by ladle, for a further 18 minutes. If the milk and cream run out, use hot water instead.

Pick out a grain of rice and squeeze it between your fingers. As soon as there is only a speck of hard white in the centre take the rice pudding off the heat and stir in the butter. Add a little more hot milk or hot water to slacken the rice slightly.

Cover and rest for 3 minutes. Stir the rice briskly, check the flavour and add extra sugar, if you like.

Divide the rice between 6 bowls and serve with a large spoonful of rhubarb and syrup.

Apple crumble with honey mascarpone

Serves 6

100g (3½oz) unsalted butter

10 Cox's apples, peeled, cored and cut into quarters, kept in water with the juice of 1 lemon

1 vanilla pod

2 bay leaves

1 tsp cinnamon powder or 1 cinnamon stick, crushed

1 star anise, crushed

pinch of ground ginger

200g (7oz) raisins

70g (2½oz) demerara sugar

200ml (7fl oz) Vin Santo

Crumble topping

150g (5½oz) blanched almonds, finely chopped

150g (5½oz) plain flour

150g (5½oz) caster sugar

150g (5½oz) unsalted butter, softened

Honey mascarpone

3 tbsp clear honey

250g (9oz) mascarpone cheese

Adding Vin Santo dessert wine to the apples and using almonds in the crumble topping gives this most English of desserts a fragrant Italian twist. Continue the theme by serving the crumble with some mascarpone cream cheese sweetened with a little honey.

Melt 70g (2½oz) of the butter in a large heavy-based saucepan. Drain the apple and tip into the saucepan. Scrape the seeds from the vanilla pod and add to the saucepan along with the bay leaves, spices and raisins. Stir with a wooden spoon and fry briefly over a high heat.

Stir in the sugar and reduce the heat to medium. Allow the sugar to caramelize to a rich toffee colour. Add the Vin Santo. Reduce the heat to minimum and stew slowly for 15–20 minutes until the apples are soft. Mix in the remaining butter. Set the stewed apple aside and pick out the bay leaves and spices.

To make the crumble topping, combine the almonds, flour and sugar in a bowl. Rub in the butter by hand or with an electrical food mixer until the mixture resembles breadcrumbs.

Reheat the stewed apple and divide it between 6 heatproof bowls. Cover with a 1cm (½in) layer of crumble topping and gently pat down. Put the crumbles under a grill on a medium heat for 3–5 minutes. (Alternatively, preheat the oven to 180°C/350°F/gas mark 4. Tip the cold apple into a baking dish, top with the crumble mixture and bake for 30–40 minutes until slightly browned.)

While the topping browns under the grill, stir the honey into the mascarpone.

Serve the apple crumble piping hot with a large spoonful of honey mascarpone.

Panettone bread-and-butter pudding

Serves 6–8

100g (3½oz) unsalted butter

1 large panettone, about 500g
(1lb 2oz), cut into 1cm (½in) slices,
crusts removed

100g (3½oz) light brown
soft sugar

300ml (½ pint) double cream

150ml (¼ pint) whole milk

1 vanilla pod

3 large free-range eggs, plus
1 large free-range egg yolk

caster sugar, to taste

Toffee sauce

125g (4½oz) caster sugar

125ml (4fl oz) water

250ml (9fl oz) double cream

Panettone is a traditional Italian bread full of dried fruits.
It has a natural sweetness and resembles brioche in texture.
Although bread-and-butter pudding is a very British recipe,
the concept of using old bread in a dessert to save waste
resonates with the Italian way of thinking.

Preheat the oven to 110°C/225°F/gas mark ¼. Grease the base
and sides of a baking dish, about 20 x 25cm (8 x 10in).

Spread all the slices of panettone with the remaining butter
and cover the bottom of the tray with a tightly packed layer of
panettone. Sprinkle half the brown sugar on top. Repeat with
a second layer of panettone, again ensuring there are no gaps
between the slices. Set the dish aside.

Pour the cream and milk into a heavy-bottomed saucepan, add
the seeds from the vanilla pod and bring to a simmer over a
medium heat. Beat the eggs and egg yolk in a mixing bowl.
Gradually pour in the boiling milk, whisking. Transfer back to
the saucepan and cook slowly over a low heat, whisking
continuously, for about 5 minutes until the custard thickens.
Then whisk in a little caster sugar to sweeten the custard.

Remove the custard from the heat and pour over the
panettone. Pat down the bread with a spoon. Leave to stand
for 3–4 minutes, shaking the dish occasionally so the custard
has a chance to permeate right through to the bottom layer.

To cook the pudding, put the baking dish into the preheated
oven and bake for 40–60 minutes or until the custard has set.

When the pudding has been in the oven for 40 minutes, make
the toffee sauce. Put the sugar and water in a saucepan over a
medium heat and stir. Once the syrup comes to the boil, stop
stirring. After about 5 minutes simmering, the syrup will start
to caramelize. Once the caramel is a rich deep toffee colour,
remove from the heat and add a slow thin stream of cream.
The caramel will bubble up at first and release steam before
subsiding. Stir to produce a smooth toffee sauce.

Serve the panettone bread-and-butter pudding straight from
the dish with a generous helping of toffee sauce.

Pancakes with mascarpone and golden syrup

Serving these pancakes with mascarpone gives them a unique Italian twist. I'd recommend adding slices of fresh orange, too, as they go well with the cheese and cut through the sweetness of the golden syrup.

Serves 4

175ml (6fl oz) buttermilk
1 large free-range egg, beaten
15g (½oz) unsalted butter, melted
50g (1¾oz) tapioca flour
25g (1oz) fine cornmeal
1 tsp cinnamon (optional)
pinch of salt
1 tsp bicarbonate of soda
a knob of clarified butter (the clear golden liquid part of melted butter)
4 tbsp mascarpone cheese
4 tbsp golden syrup

Mix together the buttermilk, beaten egg and melted butter in a large mixing bowl until smooth.

Sift the dry ingredients together and add slowly into the wet mixture. Don't worry if the mixture is a little lumpy.

Heat a heavy-based, nonstick frying pan until very hot, then reduce the heat to medium. Oil the frying pan with the clarified butter, then spoon one large tbsp of batter into the pan to make rounds approximately 8cm (3½in) in diameter.

Cook until bubbles start to rise to the surface of the pancake and burst. At this point flip the pancake over and cook the other side until golden brown. Continue to cook the pancakes until all the batter is used. Keep the cooked pancakes warm.

Serve with a dessertspoonful of mascarpone and a liberal drizzle of golden syrup.

Tiramisu with candied nuts

Tiramisu, which translates as 'pick me up', is undoubtedly the most popular of Italian desserts. Full of roasted coffee, mascarpone and good Italian chocolate, it's the perfect dessert to round off an Italian feast. Serve with candied nuts to lend sweetness to the coffee and follow with a slice of orange to refresh the palette.

Serves 6–8

450ml (¾ pint) double cream

1 vanilla pod

250g (9oz) mascarpone cheese

85g (3oz) caster sugar

50ml (2fl oz) Marsala or Tia Maria

25g (1oz) caster sugar, or to taste

500ml (18fl oz) hot strong fresh filter coffee

1 packet of ladyfinger biscuits (boudoir or Savoiardi sponge fingers)

70g (2½oz) good-quality chocolate (70 per cent cocoa solids), grated

To serve

24 sugared almonds

1 large orange, cut into 6–8 slices

Pour the cream into a mixing bowl. Scrape in the vanilla seeds and whisk to form soft peaks.

Beat the mascarpone and sugar together with a wooden spoon until smooth and softened. Fold in the whipped cream. Taste and add extra sugar if necessary. Set aside.

Stir the alcohol and sugar into the coffee. Check that the flavour is neither too bitter nor too sweet. Dip each biscuit in the coffee. Arrange a layer of ladyfingers in the base of a china or glass dish. Press down to check that the sponge fingers are well softened.

Spread a 1cm- (½in-) layer of the mascarpone–cream mixture over the sponge fingers, right up to the sides of the dish. Add another layer of soaked ladyfingers and cover with a final even layer of mascarpone, smoothing up to the sides again. Sprinkle the grated chocolate over the top.

Serve each portion of the tiramisu with a few sugared almonds and a slice of orange to refresh the palette.

Lavender pannacotta

Pannacotta is a simple, easy-to-make Italian dessert, which makes it a great choice for serving at dinner parties. Lavender, with its natural relaxant properties and subtle flavour, adds a delicate floral suggestion to this dessert.

Serves 6

1.3 litres (2¼ pints) double cream
finely grated rind of 1 unwaxed lemon
20g (¾oz) lavender on the stalk, plus extra to decorate
2 vanilla pods
4 sheets of leaf gelatine
200ml (7fl oz) whole milk
150g (5½oz) icing sugar
redcurrants to decorate (optional)

Pour the cream into a medium saucepan. Add the lemon rind and lavender stalks. Scrape the seeds from the vanilla pods and add these to the saucepan along with the pods. Bring the cream to the boil over a medium heat. Reduce the heat and simmer the cream until it has reduced by one third (about 10 minutes). Remove from the heat and set aside to infuse.

Soak the gelatine in the milk until the sheets are soft and bendy, then remove them to a plate using a slotted spoon. Pour the milk into a medium saucepan and heat to a simmer. Whisk in the icing sugar and the set-aside gelatine.

Add the milk mixture to the cream and combine. Pass through a sieve into a pouring jug. Pour the mixture evenly into 6 glass bowls or large dariole moulds (200–250ml/7–9fl oz each). Leave to set in a refrigerator overnight.

When you're ready to serve, run a little hot water over the bottom of each bowl or mould and gently ease the pannacotta away from the sides. Turn on to plates and serve with a little fresh lavender and some redcurrants, if you like.

Wild strawberry and Champagne jelly

Serves 5

Strawberry syrup

200g (7oz) large strawberries, hulled and chopped

250g (9oz) caster sugar

Champagne jelly

700ml (1 ¼ pints) Champagne or Prosecco

1 vanilla pod

9 sheets of leaf gelatine, soaked in cold water until softened

400g (14oz) wild strawberries, hulled

To serve

125g (4½ oz) mixed summer berries

icing sugar for dusting

5 sprigs of mint

There's no better flavour combination than strawberries and champagne. Wild strawberries, smaller and sweeter than the cultivated varieties, work especially well in this dessert. They are widely available in the UK in April and May.

To make the strawberry syrup, put the chopped strawberries and 140g (5oz) of the caster sugar into a heatproof bowl. Cover with clingfilm and sit over a saucepan of simmering water for 30–45 minutes, making sure that the bowl is not touching the water.

When the strawberries have released their juice and the caster sugar has dissolved to form a clear strawberry syrup, pass through a sieve into a jug and set aside in the refrigerator.

Meanwhile, pour the Champagne into a saucepan and bring to a simmer over a low heat. Scrape the seeds from the vanilla pod and add them to the Champagne. Whisk in the remaining caster sugar and the gelatine. Continue stirring until the sugar has dissolved and the gelatine has melted. Set aside to cool.

When cooled slightly, pour in just enough jelly to cover the bottom of 5 large dariole moulds. Arrange a layer of wild strawberries in the jelly and put in the refrigerator to set.

When the jelly is firm, pour in more to cover the strawberries and return to the refrigerator. When set, arrange another single layer of wild strawberries on top and pour in more jelly to cover. Continue layering wild strawberries and jelly, chilling to set each time, until the moulds are full. Leave in the refrigerator overnight.

Before serving, lightly toss the summer berries in the strawberry syrup. To release the wild strawberry and Champagne jellies, run a little hot water over the base of each mould and gently pull the jelly away from the side. Turn out on to dessert plates. Decorate with the summer berries, a light dusting of icing sugar and the mint.

Meringue with summer berries

Makes 18 meringues

Meringue

225g (8oz) caster sugar

6 tbsp water

4 free-range egg whites

1 tbsp boiling water

1 tsp white wine vinegar

Fruit syrup

425g (15oz) strawberries, hulled

150g (5½oz) caster sugar

1 punnet each of raspberries, blueberries, blackberries and strawberries

Chantilly cream

350ml (12fl oz) double cream

40g (1½oz) caster sugar

2 vanilla pods

Meringue is made from a simple combination of egg white and sugar. To prevent waste, why not use the egg yolks for a carbonara sauce? The secret of cooking meringue is to do so on a very low heat. Some chefs don't even cook them in a conventional oven – they cook them in a hot cupboard where serving plates are kept warm!

Preheat the oven to 110°C/225°F/gas mark ¼.

For the meringue, put the sugar and water in a heavy-based saucepan and bring to the boil. Use a sugar thermometer to judge when the syrup reaches 120°C (250°F). Remove from the heat.

Meanwhile, whisk the egg whites with an electric food mixer on high speed until peaks start to form. Continue to whisk while adding a steady stream of the hot sugar syrup. Add the boiling water and vinegar and keep whisking until the meringue is cool, shiny and smooth and forms very stiff spikes.

Line 2 baking sheets with baking paper. Use a large metal spoon to scoop up a neat oval mound of meringue and another spoon to slip it on to the baking sheet. Repeat with the rest of the meringue mixture, leaving a 5cm (2in) gap between the meringues.

Bake for 1 hour. Then open the oven door for 5 minutes. Close again and bake until the meringues are dry and crisp (30–60 minutes).

To make a strawberry syrup, follow the method on the facing page. Set aside to cool before stirring in the berries.

To prepare the Chantilly cream, pour the cream into a mixing bowl and add the sugar. Scrape in the seeds from the vanilla pods. Whisk until the cream forms soft peaks.

Serve 2 meringues to each person with a dollop of Chantilly cream and 1 or 2 spoonfuls of dressed berries. To decorate, drizzle fruit syrup over the meringues and around the plates.

Strawberry cheesecake

**Serves 12 as a dessert
or 8 as afternoon tea**

250g (9oz) digestive biscuits

125g (4½oz) butter, melted

3 free-range eggs

140g (5oz) caster sugar

juice and finely grated rind of
2 unwaxed lemons

4 sheets of leaf gelatine, soaked
in cold water until softened

350g (12oz) cream cheese

425ml (15fl oz) double cream

Strawberry topping

500g (1lb 2oz) strawberries, hulled
and chopped

150g (5½oz) caster sugar

1½ sheets of leaf gelatine, soaked
in cold water until softened

This dessert is a real crowd-pleaser and is great as an after-barbecue sweet accompanied by a glass of Prosecco. There's no need to bake this cheesecake as the gelatine holds the structure together.

To make the strawberry topping, follow the method for preparing a strawberry syrup in Wild strawberry and Champagne jelly (*see* page 216). When the syrup is ready, pour a little into a jug and set aside to use as decoration later. Add the gelatine to the remaining hot syrup and whisk vigorously until melted. Set aside to cool but not set.

To prepare the base, reduce the biscuits to crumbs in a food processor. Pour in just enough butter to bind the crumbs.

Place a 25cm (10in) round, straight-sided cake tin without its base on a baking sheet lined with baking paper. Press the crumb mixture firmly into the bottom of the ring with your fingers. Set aside in the refrigerator to firm up.

To make the filling, whisk the eggs and sugar together in an electric food mixer until thoroughly mixed. Warm the lemon juice in a small saucepan over a low heat. Add the drained gelatine and whisk until melted. Stir into the eggs.

Vigorously beat the cream cheese with a wooden spoon until softened and smooth. Beat in the lemon rind with the egg and lemon mixture and set aside.

In a separate mixing bowl, whisk the cream to soft peaks with an electric hand whisk. Beat 1 tbsp of the whipped cream into the cream cheese to slacken it before folding in the rest.

Tip the cream cheese filling over the biscuit base and level the top with a spatula. Return to the refrigerator to set. If the top seems uneven when the cheesecake is firm, gently slide off the cake tin and scrape the surface smooth and level. Replace the cake tin and gently pour the cooled strawberry topping over the top. Return to the refrigerator to set.

When ready to serve, remove the cake tin. Slice the cheesecake and decorate with a drizzle of strawberry syrup.

index

Agnolotti of roasted onion, pine nuts, rocket and Anya potatoes 40

aïoli, lemon: Sicilian fisherman's stew with lemon aïoli and tarragon 118

almonds
  Grilled rainbow trout with orange and watercress salad and toasted flaked almonds 102
  Tiramisu with candied nuts 211

anchovies
  Lemon sole with anchovy and caper butter sauce 112
  Slow-roasted shoulder of lamb with spring greens in an anchovy and rosemary dressing 87

apples
  Apple crumble with honey mascarpone 207
  Cheeky-chop sandwich filled with spinach and ricotta with cinnamon roasted apples 72
  Shaved fennel, apple and Pecorino Sardo salad 171

apricots, dried: Rolled loin of pork stuffed with dried apricot and sage 68

Arborio rice
  Arborio rice pudding with rhubarb 206
  Basic risotto bianco 45

artichokes
  Lasagnette with Parma ham, artichokes and mascarpone 31
  Pan-fried seabass supreme with potato and artichoke al forno and olive tapenade 107
  Polenta-crusted rack of lamb with potato and artichoke al forno 89

asparagus: Ravioli soleil with asparagus and pecorino 42

balsamic vinegar
  Ham hock, roast chestnut and balsamic vinegar risotto with crisp fried sage leaves 48
  Pan-fried calves' livers with olive-oil mash, balsamic figs and crisp pancetta 83

basil
  Mozzarella, sun-blushed tomatoes and basil 167
  Octopus carpaccio with tomato salsa and basil 164
  Simple tomato salad with basil and grissini 167
  Tagliarini with lobster, lemon, parsley and purple basil 34

beef
  Italian beefburgers with tomato relish 134
  Salami misti 156
  Slow-braised shin of beef in red wine with oozy polenta and mustard fruits 78
  T-bone Florentine 77
  Tagliatelle with minute steaks rolled with pecorino and thyme 26

beetroot: Spatchcocked poussin with beetroot, spring greens and herb mascarpone 90

blackberries

Meringue with summer berries 217

Pot-roasted pheasant with mixed fruits 93

blueberries: Meringue with summer berries 217

breads
  Basic bread dough 178
  Boned leg of spring lamb, rubbed with rosemary and garlic marinade with flatbreads and Moroccan couscous 131
  Burnt rolls 195
  Chicken liver pâté with fig chutney and lavosh 96
  Chorizo sausage and red wine risotto with gorgonzola crostini 47
  Ciabatta bread 189
  Crostini misti 167
  Fennel and polenta bread 180
  Ferment (starter dough) 190
  Flatbread pizzas 146
  Grissini 193
  Lavosh (Armenian flatbread) 187
  Lobster curry with fennel and polenta bread 122
  Mini focaccia 194
  Panettone bread-and-butter pudding 208
  Rosemary and raisin bread 185
  Rye sourdough bread 191
  Simple tomato salad with basil and grissini 168
  Smoked mackerel paté with burnt rolls 162
  Tomato bread cones 186
  Turmeric flatbreads 186

broad beans: Chervil gnocchi with broad beans and mint 59

broccoli: Steamed halibut with purple sprouting broccoli and black olives 110

butternut squash: Chintora filled with butternut squash and black figs 33

calves' livers: Pan-fried calves' livers with olive-oil mash, balsamic figs and crisp pancetta 83

capers: Lemon sole with anchovy and caper butter sauce 112

Cappelletti filled with prawns and chilli 36

carnaroli
  Basic risotto bianco 45
  Chorizo sausage and red wine risotto with Gorgonzola crostini 47

cauliflower: Risotto with purple cauliflower and Amalfi lemon 52

celeriac: Pan-seared scallops with celeriac mash, Swiss chard and pancetta 124

Champagne: Wild strawberry and Champagne jelly 216

Cheeky Chops (later Fifteen Foundation) 72

cheese
  Tiramisu with candied nuts 211
  see also gorgonzola; mascarpone; mozzarella; Parmesan; pecorino; ricotta

cheesecake: Strawberry cheesecake 218

Chervil gnocchi with broad beans and mint 59

chestnuts: Ham hock, roast chestnut and balsamic vinegar risotto with crisp fried sage leaves 48

chicken: Minted gnocchi with chicken and peas 57

Chicken liver pâté with fig chutney and lavosh 96

chillies
  Barbecued squid with chilli jam dip 145
  Cappelletti filled with prawns and chilli 36

Chintora filled with butternut squash and black figs 33

Chocolate fondant-soufflé 205

Chorizo sausage and red wine risotto with gorgonzola crostini 47

Ciabatta bread 189

cinnamon: Cheeky-chop sandwich filled with spinach and ricotta with cinnamon roasted apples 72

cippolini onions: Easter leg of kid with cippolini onions and mint 85

clams
  Potato and lemon gnocchi with mussels and clams 60
  Seafood lasagne 115
  Sicilian fisherman's stew with lemon aïoli and tarragon 118

cod
  Cod with rosemary-salted chips and tartare sauce 111
  Fish Pie 117
  Salt cod al forno 125

coleslaw: Grilled pigeon breast with coleslaw 157

courgettes: Grilled salmon with fennel, pine nut and crème fraîche salad and zucchini fritti 104

couscous: Boned leg of spring lamb, rubbed with rosemary and garlic marinade with flatbreads and Moroccan couscous 131

crab: Risotto with crab, cherry tomatoes and tarragon 50

crème fraîche: Grilled salmon with fennel, pine nut and crème fraîche salad and zucchini fritti 104

crostini
  Chorizo sausage and red wine risotto with gorgonzola crostini 47
  Crostini misti 167

duck: Roasted duck breast in holy-wine sauce with pomegranate seeds 92

eels: Risotto with smoked eel and sorrel 49

eggs
  Basic egg pasta dough 25
  Tuna confit with soft-boiled egg and pancetta dressing 161

fennel

Fennel and polenta bread 180
Grilled salmon with fennel, pine nut and crème fraîche salad and zucchini fritti 104
Lobster curry with fennel and polenta bread 122
Monkfish with braised fennel, salami and salsa rossa piccante 114
Shaved fennel, apple and Pecorino Sardo salad 171
Ferment (starter dough) 190
figs
Chicken liver pâté with fig chutney and lavosh 96
Chintora filled with butternut squash and black figs 33
Pan-fried calves' livers with olive-oil mash, balsamic figs and crisp pancetta 83
fish
preparing 101
see also individual names of fish
focaccia: Mini focaccia 194

garlic
Boned leg of spring lamb, rubbed with rosemary and garlic marinade with flatbreads and Moroccan couscous 131
Red mullet with grilled spring garlic 142
girolles: Potato and parsley gnocchi with summer girolles and pecorino 62
gnocchi 22
Basic gnocchi 55
Chervil gnocchi with broad beans and mint 59
Gnocchi with gorgonzola and walnuts 61
Minted gnocchi with chicken and peas 57
My award-winning tomato gnocchi with oxtail stew 56
Lemon gnocchi with mussels and clams 60
Potato and parsley gnocchi with summer girolles and pecorino 62
goat: Easter leg of kid with cippolini onions and mint 85
golden syrup: Pancakes with mascarpone and golden syrup 210
gorgonzola
Chorizo sausage and red wine risotto with gorgonzola crostini 47
Gnocchi with gorgonzola and walnuts 61
green beans: Whole baked seabream with green beans and oregano dressing 106
grissini
Grissini 193
Simple tomato salad with basil and grissini 167

haddock: Fish Pie 117
hake: Fish Pie 117
halibut: Steamed halibut with purple sprouting broccoli and black olives 110
ham
Ham hock, roast chestnut and balsamic vinegar risotto with crisp fried sage leaves 48
Lasagnette with Parma ham, artichokes and mascarpone 31
Mozzarella salad with prosciutto di Parma,

melon and pistachios 153
herbs
Fillets of seabass stuffed with summer herbs 137
Spatchcocked poussin with beetroot, spring greens and herb mascarpone 90
see also individual herbs
holy wine: Roasted duck breast in holy-wine sauce with pomegranate seeds 92
honey
Apple crumble with honey mascarpone 207
Confit of rabbit with honey-roasted parsnips 94
horseradish: Pan-fried fillet of beef with roasted summer vegetables and freshly grated horseradish 80

John Dory: Roasted John Dory with lemon thyme, Roosevelt potatoes, taggiasca olives and salsa verde 109
juniper berries: Roast venison with juniper gravy 97

lamb
Boned leg of spring lamb, rubbed with rosemary and garlic marinade with flatbreads and Moroccan couscous 131
Polenta-crusted rack of lamb with potato and artichoke al forno 89
Roman spring lamb casserole 86
Slow-roasted shoulder of lamb with spring greens in an anchovy and rosemary dressing 87
lasagne: Seafood lasagne 115
Lasagnette with Parma ham, artichokes and mascarpone 31
Lavender pannacotta 215
lavosh
Chicken liver pâté with fig chutney and lavosh 96
Lavosh (Armenian flatbread) 187
Lemon sole with anchovy and caper butter sauce 112
lemon thyme: Roasted John Dory with lemon thyme, Roosevelt potatoes, taggiasca olives and salsa verde 109
lemons
Amalfi lemon curd tart 200
Fried whitebait with lemon, parsley and paprika mayo 160
Lemon and polenta cake 202
Potato and lemon gnocchi with mussels and clams 60
Risotto with purple cauliflower and Amalfi lemon 52
Tagliarini with lobster, lemon, parsley and purple basil 34
Whole seabream stuffed with lemon rosemary and basil 141
Linguini with fresh tomatoes, green olives and mozzarella 38
lobster
Lobster curry with fennel and polenta bread 122

Tagliarini with lobster, lemon, parsley and purple basil 34
mackerel: Smoked mackerel paté with burnt rolls 162
mascarpone
Apple crumble with honey mascarpone 207
Lasagnette with Parma ham, artichokes and mascarpone 31
Pancakes with mascarpone and golden syrup 210
Spatchcocked poussin with beetroot, spring greens and herb mascarpone 90
Tiramisu with candied nuts 211
meat
buying and cuts 67
see also individual types of meat
meatballs: Big Al's spicy pork meatballs with stracci 29
melons: Mozzarella salad with prosciutto di Parma, melon and pistachios 153
Meringue with summer berries 217
milk: Boned shoulder of pork cooked in milk and peaches 70
mint
Chervil gnocchi with broad beans and mint 59
Easter leg of kid with cippolini onions and mint 85
Garden peas, pecorino, mint and crispy pancetta 167
Minted gnocchi with chicken and peas 57
Monkfish with braised fennel, salami and salsa rossa piccante 114
Mostarda di Cremona: Slow-braised shin of beef in red wine with oozy polenta and mustard fruits 78
mozzarella
Linguini with fresh tomatoes, green olives and mozzarella 38
Mozzarella, sun-blushed tomatoes and basil 167
Mozzarella salad with prosciutto di Parma, melon and pistachios 153
mushrooms: Potato and parsley gnocchi with summer girolles and pecorino 62
mussels
Mussels in salsa rossa piccante 121
Potato and lemon gnocchi with mussels and clams 60
Seafood lasagne 115
Sicilian fisherman's stew with lemon aïoli and tarragon 118
mustard
Roast belly of pork with mustard mash and salsa dragoncello 71
Slow-braised shin of beef in red wine with oozy polenta and mustard fruits 78

Octopus carpaccio with tomato salsa and basil 164
olive oil
Pan-fried calves' livers with olive-oil mash, balsamic figs and crisp pancetta 83
Seared swordfish with panzanella salad and tomato oil 105
olives

Black olive tapenade 167
Linguini with fresh tomatoes, green olives and mozzarella 38
Pan-fried seabass supreme with potato and artichoke al forno and olive tapenade 107
Roasted John Dory with lemon thyme, Roosevelt potatoes, taggiasca olives and salsa verde 109
Steamed halibut with purple sprouting broccoli and black olives 110
onions
Agnolotti of roasted onion, pine nuts, rocket and Anya potatoes 40
Easter leg of kid with cippolini onions and mint 85
Seafood spiedini with onions and peppers 144
oranges: Grilled rainbow trout with orange and watercress salad and toasted flaked almonds 102
oregano: Whole baked seabream with green beans and oregano dressing 106
oxtail: My award-winning tomato gnocchi with oxtail stew 56

Pancakes with mascarpone and golden syrup 210
pancetta
Garden peas, pecorino, mint and crispy pancetta 167
Pan-fried calves' livers with olive-oil mash, balsamic figs and crisp pancetta 83
Pan-seared scallops with celeriac mash, Swiss chard and pancetta 124
Tuna confit with soft-boiled egg and pancetta dressing 161
Panettone bread-and-butter pudding 208
pannacotta: Lavender pannacotta 215
panzanella: Seared swordfish with panzanella salad and tomato oil 105
paprika: Fried whitebait with lemon, parsley and paprika mayo 160
Parmesan: Risotto with purple cauliflower and Amalfi lemon 52
parsley
Fried whitebait with lemon, parsley and paprika mayo 160
Potato and parsley gnocchi with summer girolles and pecorino 62
Spatchcocked poussin with beetroot, spring greens and herb mascarpone 90
Tagliarini with lobster, lemon, parsley and purple basil 34
parsnips: Confit of rabbit with honey-roasted parsnips 94
pasta see individual types of pasta
pasta dough: Basic egg pasta dough 25
peaches: Boned shoulder of pork cooked in milk and peaches 70
peas
Garden peas, pecorino, mint and crispy pancetta 167
Minted gnocchi with chicken and peas 57
pecorino
Garden peas, pecorino, mint and crispy

pancetta 167
Potato and parsley gnocchi with summer girolles and pecorino 62
Ravioli soleil with asparagus and pecorino 42
Shaved fennel, apple and Pecorino Sardo salad 171
Tagliatelle with minute steaks rolled with pecorino and thyme 26
Penne with sun-blushed tomato pesto 43
peppers
Rigatoni with Italian sausages and grilled red peppers 28
Seafood spiedini with onions and peppers 144
pesto: Penne with sun-blushed tomato pesto 43
pheasant: Pot-roasted pheasant with mixed fruits 93
pigeon: Grilled pigeon breast with coleslaw 157
pine nuts
Agnolotti of roasted onion, pine nuts, rocket and Anya potatoes 40
Grilled salmon with fennel, pine nut and crème fraîche salad and zucchini fritti 104
pistachios: Mozzarella salad with prosciutto di Parma, melon and pistachios 153
pizzas: Flatbread pizzas 146
polenta
Fennel and polenta bread 180
Lemon and polenta cake 202
Lobster curry with fennel and polenta bread 122
Polenta-crusted rack of lamb with potato and artichoke al forno 89
Slow-braised shin of beef in red wine with oozy polenta and mustard fruits 78
pomegranates: Roasted duck breast in holy-wine sauce with pomegranate seeds 92
pork
Barbecued belly pork with salsa verde 136
Big Al's spicy pork meatballs with stracci 29
Boned shoulder of pork cooked in milk and peaches 70
Cheeky-chop sandwich filled with spinach and ricotta with cinnamon roasted apples 72
Pork stew with spicy Italian sausage 76
Roast belly of pork with mustard mash and salsa dragoncello 71
Rolled loin of pork stuffed with dried apricot and sage 68
Sliced pork with tuna sauce 154
see also ham; pancetta; prosciutto; salami
potatoes 22
Agnolotti of roasted onion, pine nuts, rocket and Anya potatoes 40
Basic gnocci 55
Cod with rosemary-salted chips and tartare sauce 111
Fish Pie 117
Pan-fried calves' livers with olive-oil mash, balsamic figs and crisp pancetta 83
Pan-fried seabass supreme with potato and artichoke al forno and olive tapenade 107
Pan-seared scallops with celeriac mash, Swiss chard and pancetta 124
Polenta-crusted rack of lamb with potato

and artichoke al forno 89
Potato and lemon gnocchi with mussels and clams 60
Potato and parsley gnocchi with summer girolles and pecorino 62
Roast belly of pork with mustard mash and salsa dragoncello 71
Roasted John Dory with lemon thyme, Roosevelt potatoes, taggiasca olives and salsa verde 109
Smoked salmon with potato salad and homemade salad cream 165
poussin: Spatchcocked poussin with beetroot, spring greens and herb mascarpone 90
prawns
Cappelletti filled with prawns and chilli 36
Fish Pie 117
Seafood lasagne 115
Seafood spiedini with onions and peppers 144
Sicilian fisherman's stew with lemon aïoli and tarragon 118
prosciutto
Mozzarella salad with prosciutto di Parma, melon and pistachios 153
Salami misti 156

rabbit
Confit of rabbit with honey-roasted parsnips 94
Ravioli pincia with slow-roasted rabbit filling 32
raisins: Rosemary and raisin bread 185
raspberries
Meringue with summer berries 217
Raspberry frangipane tart 203
ravioli
Ravioli pincia with slow-roasted rabbit filling 32
Ravioli soleil with asparagus and pecorino 42
red mullet
Red mullet with grilled spring garlic 142
Sicilian fisherman's stew with lemon aïoli and tarragon 118
rhubarb: Arborio rice pudding with rhubarb 206
rice see Arborio rice
ricotta: Cheeky-chop sandwich filled with spinach and ricotta with cinnamon roasted apples 72
Rigatoni with Italian sausages and grilled red peppers 28
risottos
Basic risotto bianco 45
Chorizo sausage and red wine risotto with gorgonzola crostini 47
Ham hock, roast chestnut and balsamic vinegar risotto with crisp fried sage leaves 48
Risotto with crab, cherry tomatoes and tarragon 50
Risotto with purple cauliflower and Amalfi lemon 52
Risotto with smoked eel and sorrel 49
rocket: Agnolotti of roasted onion, pine nuts, rocket and Anya potatoes 40

rosemary
Boned leg of spring lamb, rubbed with rosemary and garlic marinade with flatbreads and Moroccan couscous 131
Cod with rosemary-salted chips and tartare sauce 111
Rosemary and raisin bread 185
Slow-roasted shoulder of lamb with spring greens in an anchovy and rosemary dressing 87
Whole seabream stuffed with lemon rosemary and basil 141
Rye sourdough bread 191

sage
Ham hock, roast chestnut and balsamic vinegar risotto with crisp fried sage leaves 48
Rolled loin of pork stuffed with dried apricot and sage 68
salad cream: Smoked salmon with potato salad and homemade salad cream 165
salads 150
Funky leaf salad 173
Grilled rainbow trout with orange and watercress salad and toasted flaked almonds 102
Grilled salmon with fennel, pine nut and crème fraîche salad and zucchini fritti 104
Mozzarella salad with prosciutto di Parma, melon and pistachios 153
Seared swordfish with panzanella salad and tomato oil 105
Shaved fennel, apple and Pecorino Sardo salad 171
Simple tomato salad with basil and grissini 168
Smoked salmon with potato salad and homemade salad cream 165
salami
Monkfish with braised fennel, salami and salsa rossa piccante 114
Salami misti 156
salmon
Grilled salmon with fennel, pine nut and crème fraîche salad and zucchini fritti 104
Smoked salmon with potato salad and homemade salad cream 165
salsas
Barbecued belly pork with salsa verde 136
Monkfish with braised fennel, salami and salsa rossa piccante 114
Mussels in salsa rossa piccante 121
Octopus carpaccio with tomato salsa and basil 164
Roast belly of pork with mustard mash and salsa dragoncello 71
Roasted John Dory with lemon thyme, Roosevelt potatoes, taggiasca olives and salsa verde 109
Salsicca: Pork stew with spicy Italian sausage 76
Salt cod al forno 125
sardines: Grilled sardines with agra dolce dressing 159
sausages

Chorizo sausage and red wine risotto with gorgonzola crostini 47
Pork stew with spicy Italian sausage 76
Rigatoni with Italian sausages and grilled red peppers 28
scallops
Pan-seared scallops with celeriac mash, Swiss chard and pancetta 124
Seafood lasagne 115
Seafood spiedini with onions and peppers 144
seabass
Fillets of seabass stuffed with summer herbs 137
Pan-fried seabass supreme with potato and artichoke al forno and olive tapenade 107
Sicilian fisherman's stew with lemon aïoli and tarragon 118
seabream
Whole baked seabream with green beans and oregano dressing 106
Whole seabream stuffed with lemon rosemary and basil 141
sorrel: Risotto with smoked eel and sorrel 49
spiedini: Seafood spiedini with onions and peppers 144
spinach: Cheeky-chop sandwich filled with spinach and ricotta with cinnamon roasted apples 72
spring greens
Slow-roasted shoulder of lamb with spring greens in an anchovy and rosemary dressing 87
Spatchcocked poussin with beetroot, spring greens and herb mascarpone 90
squid: Barbecued squid with chilli jam dip 145
stews
My award-winning tomato gnocchi with oxtail stew 56
Pork stew with spicy Italian sausage 76
Roman spring lamb casserole 86
Sicilian fisherman's stew with lemon aïoli and tarragon 118
stracci: Big Al's spicy pork meatballs with stracci 29
strawberries
Meringue with summer berries 217
Strawberry cheesecake 218
Wild strawberry and Champagne jelly 216
Swiss chard: Pan-seared scallops with celeriac mash, Swiss chard and pancetta 124
swordfish
Seafood spiedini with onions and peppers 144
Seared swordfish with panzanella salad and tomato oil 105

Tagliarini with lobster, lemon, parsley and purple basil 34
Tagliatelle with minute steaks rolled with pecorino and thyme 26
tapenades
Black olive tapenade 167
Pan-fried seabass supreme with potato and artichoke al forno and olive tapenade 107
tarragon

Risotto with crab, cherry tomatoes and tarragon 50
Sicilian fisherman's stew with lemon aïoli and tarragon 118
tartare sauce: Cod with rosemary-salted chips and tartare sauce 111
thyme
Roasted John Dory with lemon thyme, Roosevelt potatoes, taggiasca olives and salsa verde 109
Tagliatelle with minute steaks rolled with pecorino and thyme 26
Tiramisu with candied nuts 211
tomato juice: Seared swordfish with panzanella salad and tomato oil 105
tomatoes
Italian beefburgers with tomato relish 134
Linguini with fresh tomatoes, green olives and mozzarella 38
Mozzarella, sun-blushed tomatoes and basil 167
My award-winning tomato gnocchi with oxtail stew 56
Octopus carpaccio with tomato salsa and basil 164
Penne with sun-blushed tomato pesto 43
Risotto with crab, cherry tomatoes and tarragon 50
Simple tomato salad with basil and grissini 167
Tomato bread cones 186
trout: Grilled rainbow trout with orange and watercress salad and toasted flaked almonds 102
tuna
Seafood lasagne 115
Seafood spiedini with onions and peppers 144
Sicilian fisherman's stew with lemon aïoli and tarragon 118
Sliced pork with tuna sauce 154
Tuna confit with soft-boiled egg and pancetta dressing 161
Turmeric flatbreads 186

vegetables
Mixed grilled vegetables 170
Pan-fried fillet of beef with roasted summer vegetables and freshly grated horseradish 80
see also individual vegetables
venison: Roast venison with juniper gravy 97

walnuts: Gnocchi with gorgonzola and walnuts 61
watercress: Grilled rainbow trout with orange and watercress salad and toasted flaked almonds 102
whitebait: Fried whitebait with lemon, parsley and paprika mayo 160
wine
Chorizo sausage and red wine risotto with gorgonzola crostini 47
Roasted duck breast in holy-wine sauce with pomegranate seeds 92
Slow-braised shin of beef in red wine with oozy polenta and mustard fruits 78

acknowledgements

I'd like to thank my partner Nicci and my two beautiful daughters Molly and Leah for supporting me and giving me the inspiration to make all of this possible. Thanks to my mother-in-law Dee for inspiring me to cook in the first place, and to my mum Kathleen, my brother Spencer and my two sisters Chelsea and Candy, who I love very much.

Thanks to all the chefs who trained me at Fifteen – Ben Arthur, Gennaro Contaldo, Elton Englis, Trevor Howard, Mario Magli, Andrew Parkinson, Steve Pooley, Tobie Puttock, Arthur Potts Dawson and Santos. Thanks most of all to Andy Appleton for believing in me and taking me under his wing in my last and best year at Fifteen. Legend!

Thanks to all the guys from the pub who I was fortunate enough to work with and who I love very much. They include pastry chefs Daniel Bacon, Christopher Jeffrey and Daniel Stafford; master baker Sam.May; sous chef Gareth Boothby; chefs de partie Richard Cutting, Sarah Powell, Gary Saunders and James Yallop; pot-washers Matthew Watkins and Thomas Wiffen; floor supervisors Kerry Hurst, Sarah Munday and Liz O'Shea; and floor staff Tom Johnson, Kim Phillips, Lucy Roberts, Ella Robson, Louise Seaman and Laeticia (La la).

Thanks to my agent Debbie Catchpole, and to Verity O'Brien of Fresh Partners.

Thanks to Jamie, Trevor and Sally Oliver. Thanks to Anna Jones for giving me the great idea of the ice cream van at Jamie's birthday party.

Thanks to Luke Robinson for his help and support thoughout the process of making the book and for being a great friend and sous chef. Watch this space!

Thanks to Nick Jones at the Soho House Group, to Steve Angel and Louise Holland, and to David Gleave and everyone at Liberty Wines (without you I'd never have been introduced to Italy). Thanks also to Sheila Fraser and all the Hospitality and Catering team at Ealing, Hammersmith and West London College.

Thanks to all our suppliers, especially Dave Robson for all his wonderful game. Thanks to the locals Big Frank, Kieran and Smiley for their constant support.

Thanks also to everyone at Mitchell Beazley and all the team that helped produce the book, in particular photographer Jason Lowe, food stylist Sue Henderson, designer Nicky Collings and recipe testers Marisa Viola, Vicky Musselman and Georgie Socratous.